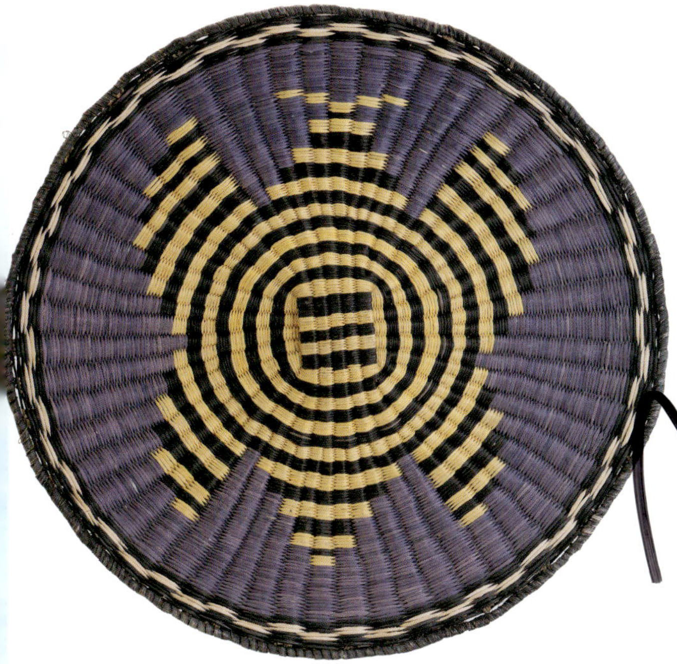

# Hold Everything!

JODY FOLWELL   DIZA SAUERS   **TERROL DEW JOHNSON**   TRISTAN READER

ANN E. MARSHALL

DIANA F. PARDUE

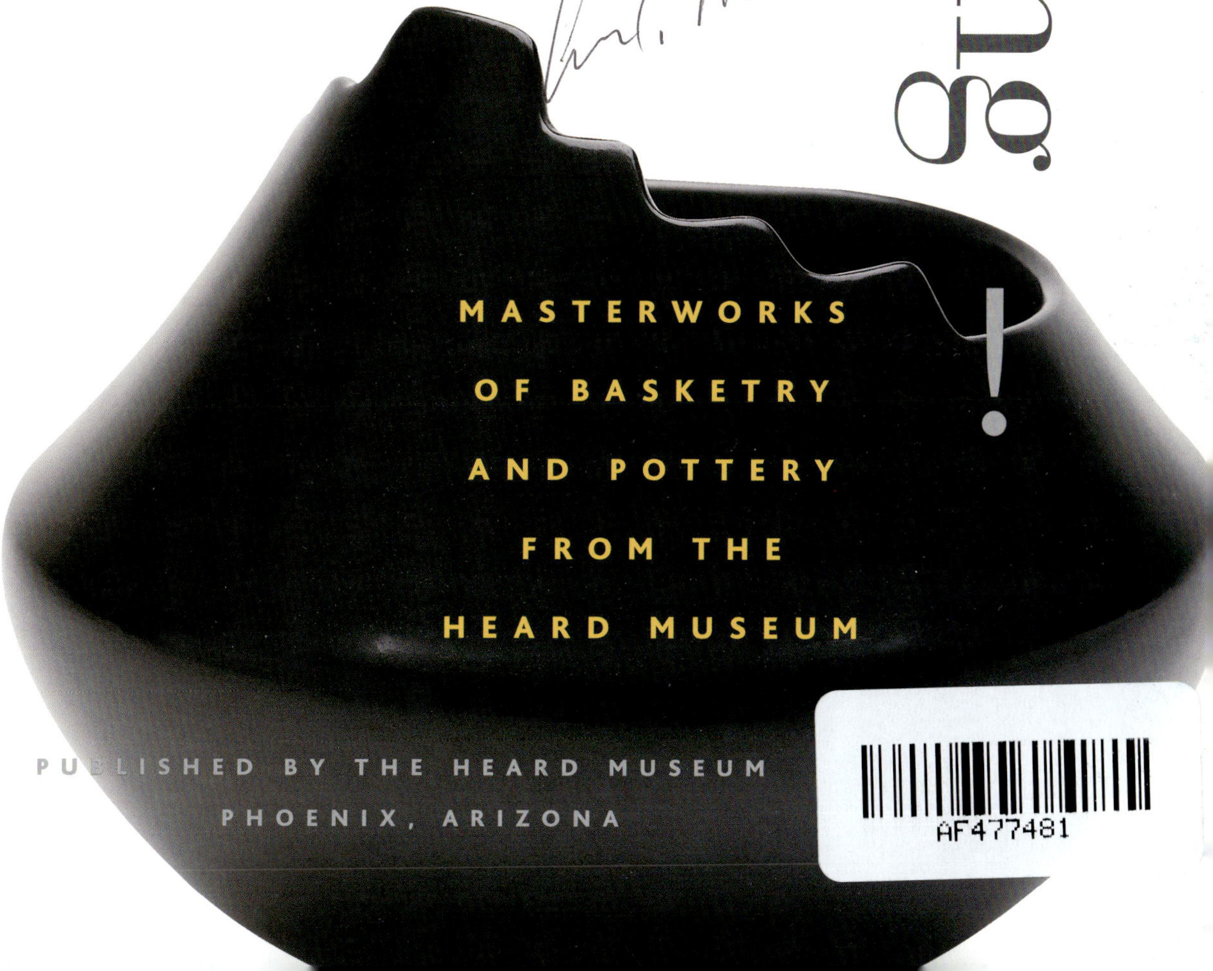

MASTERWORKS
OF BASKETRY
AND POTTERY
FROM THE
HEARD MUSEUM

PUBLISHED BY THE HEARD MUSEUM
PHOENIX, ARIZONA

ISBN 0-934351-64-2

DISTRIBUTED BY
MUSEUM OF NEW MEXICO PRESS, SANTA FE

DESIGN BY CAROL HARALSON
PHOTOS BY CRAIG SMITH
COPYEDITED BY JULIET MARTIN
COORDINATED BY LISA MACCOLLUM


PRINTED IN CHINA


Library of Congress Cataloging-in-Publication Data

Heard Museum
        Hold everything! : masterworks of basketry and
pottery from the Heard Museum collection /
by Jody Folwell ... [et al.].
        p.cm.
        Catalog of a travelling exhibition which was first
displayed at the Heard Museum between Nov. 3, 2001
and Mar. 10, 2002.
        ISBN 0-934351-64-3
        1. Indian baskets—North America—Exhibitions.
2. Indian pottery—North America—Exhibitions.
3. Indian pottery—Southwest, New—Exhibitions.
4. Indian baskets—Southwest, New—Exhibitions.
5. Heard Museum—Exhibitions. 6. Heard Museum.
I. Folwell, Jody, 1942-  II. Title.

    E98.B3 H43 2001
    704.03'97'0074--dc21
                        2001039666

PHOTOGRAPHS:

*Front cover:* Hopi, Third Mesa pictorial plaque, 1970. .5 x
14; 14 wefts/inch. Wicker with dunebroom warps and
rabbitbrush wefts with aniline dyes, yucca wrap at rim. Gift
of Mr. and Mrs. Byron Harvey III, NA-SW-HO-B-129.

*Front cover inset:* Maria and Julian Martinez, San Ildefonso
(1890-1980 and 1807-1943). Plate, 1925-1943. 3 x 14. Gift
of Madeline and Russell Warren, 3465-2.

*Back cover:* Detail. Grace Medicine Flower, Santa Clara
(b. 1938). Jar with lid, 1991. 13.5 x 6.75. Gift of John and
Rita Rye, 4110-3A,B.

*Title page:* Tina Garcia, Santa Clara (b. 1957). Jar, 1988. 7.5
x 7.5. Acquired by the donor at the Andrews Gallery in
Albuquerque, New Mexico. Given in memory of Dr. Stuart
G. Meibuhr, 4099-2; Hopi pictorial plaque at upper left
same as front cover.

*Contents page:* Nancy Youngblood, Santa Clara (b. 1955).
Jar with lid, 1995. 9.75 x 6. Gift of Dr. Eric Tack, 3828-
1A,B.

*Page 4:* Maria and Julian Martinez, San Ildefonso (1897-
1943; 1925-1943). Plate, 1925-1943. 3 x 14. Gift of
Madeline and Russell Warren, 3465-1.

*Page 5:* Navajo bowl basket, c. 1900. 3.25 x 12.5; 4
coils/inch, 11 stitches/inch. Close coiled on a two-rod-and-
bundle foundation of sumac and yucca fibers with sewing
element of sumac dyed with mineral and vegetal dyes; herringbone rim finish. Fred Harvey Fine Arts Collection,
242BA.


Dimensions are given in inches, height preceding width
followed by depth.


*Hold Everything!* is published through the generous support
of the Dr. and Mrs. Dean Nichols Publications Fund.

This publication was produced in conjunction with the
first exhibit in the Masterworks Series, *Hold Everything!
Masterworks of Basketry and Pottery from the Heard
Museum,* sponsored by SRP, Bank of America and Joel and
Lila Harnett.

Exhibit dates at the Heard Museum:
November 3, 2001, to March 10, 2002

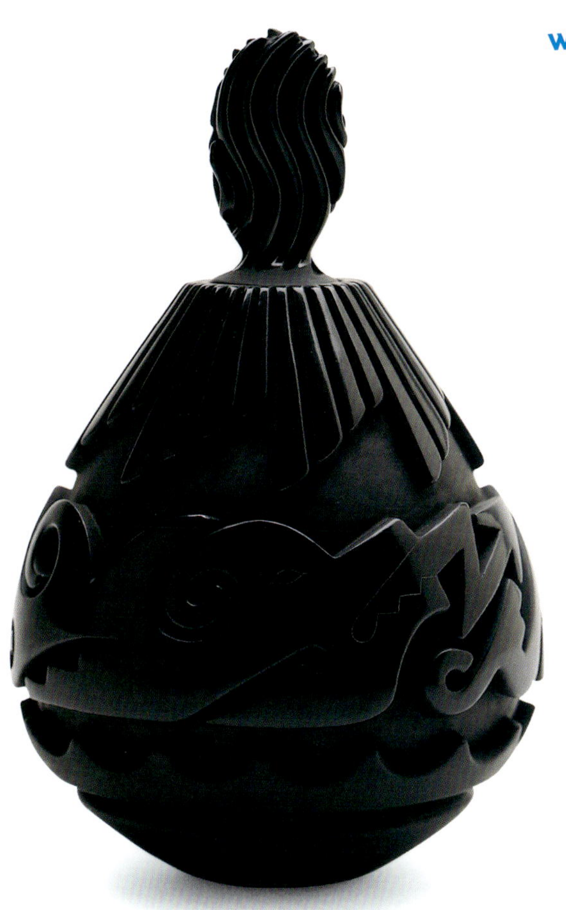

FOREWORD

# POTTERY AND BASKETS:

## Masterworks That Hold Everything

### DR. ANN E. MARSHALL

FOR MORE than a decade, the Heard Museum has been actively engaged in exploring ways to bring the "first-person" voice to the interpretation of its collections. Much of the exploration has been done through exhibits, and we have been eager to develop a publication series that brings the insights of Native artists who are interpreting the collection to a wider audience. After considering various options for creating a first-person perspective, we decided to invite a Native artist to serve as a guest curator for each of the artistic traditions being presented. This approach allows the guest curators/ artists to use the collection as a medium with which to illustrate their own views about the defining qualities of masterworks.

Since the concept of "masterworks" derives from Euro-American art historical concepts, we needed to select guest curators who are comfortable with applying this alien construct to pieces created within Native traditions that are based on different value systems. We knew at the beginning that the works selected would most likely not meet the established outsider-created art canons. As the people who actually create something, artists have a unique understanding of the nature of achievement that may be hidden within a piece.

*Hold Everything!*, the first book in the series, looks at Native containers, which for centuries have blended beauty and utility in remarkable and endless variation. In identifying a guest curator to select ceramic masterworks in the Heard collection, we sought an accomplished potter who had created a significant body of work, someone who displayed depth and variety as well as a level of artistry that had led to the production of masterworks. We were interested in an artist who had explored a variety of techniques, shapes, polishes and designs and, because of this range of accomplishment, could look with understanding and insight at the variety of ceramic work done in the American Southwest, the place where ceramic traditions have flourished for centuries. We wanted a guest curator who was a part of that artistic tradition and yet had worked in innovative ways— stretching the bounds. We selected Jody Folwell, Santa Clara, who fits the above description perfectly. An award-winning potter, she has been featured in numerous museum exhibits and gallery shows, including the comprehensive National Museum of Women in the Arts' exhibit *The Legacy of Generations: Pottery by American Indian Women* where exhibit curator Susan Peterson selected Folwell as one of the leading avant-garde potters.

When we considered whom to choose as guest curator for the Heard's basket collection, we knew the individual would have a difficult task. We were aware of several superb weavers who would do a fine job of reviewing baskets from their own traditions, but we needed someone who could review a collection containing works from across North America.

Adding to the difficulty was the fact that baskets are one of the more anonymous Native art forms. While Folwell found herself reviewing pieces, some of which were signed, from a much smaller geographic area, the guest curator of baskets would be working with traditions largely unknown to him and by unknown weavers. Given those considerations, we thought immediately of Terrol Dew Johnson, a young Tohono O'odham man who is a weaver, but whose greatest achievement has been his work with cultural revitalization of the medium, in his own community and across the country. He is the originator of the major Native American basketmakers conference and festival in the United States. Held in Arizona, the festival brings together weavers from Maine to Hawai'i, and during the year Johnson travels frequently to gatherings of weavers in their home

communities, where he has learned first hand about the many basketry traditions. The festival is part of a major movement that is the most recent chapter in the history of Native baskets in America. In a larger sense, the basket cultural revitalization groups seek to preserve language, ceremonies and traditional knowledge of the land and plants. The goal for these groups is to learn from elders and pass the knowledge along to younger people. Johnson's experience with basketweavers today as they preserve, revive and reinvigorate their cultural heritages well qualified him to develop the concept of basket masterworks within the Heard Museum collection.

When the two artists came to the museum to begin the selection process in spring 2001, they arrived with differing perspectives. Johnson had worked with the collection in the past and

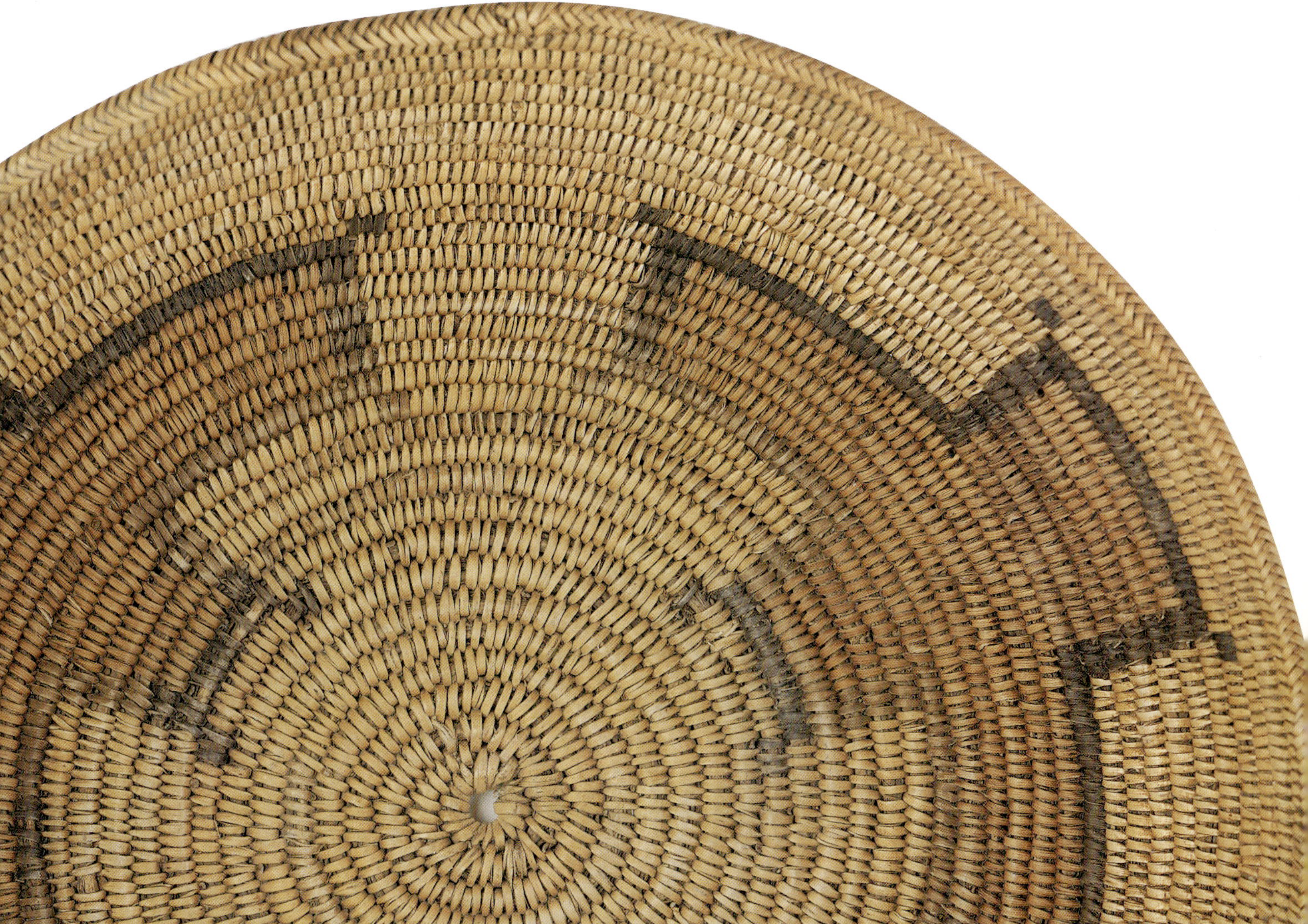

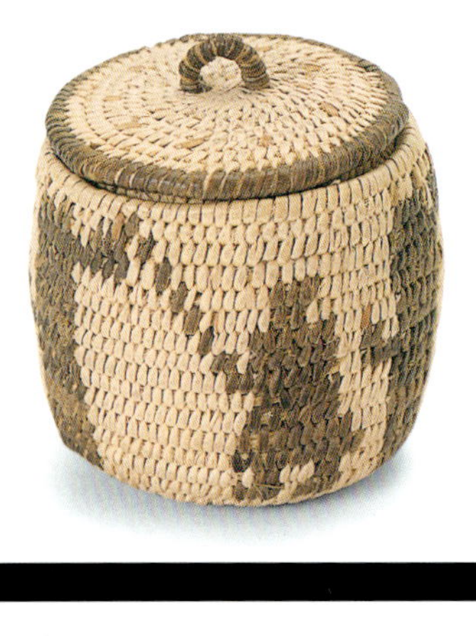
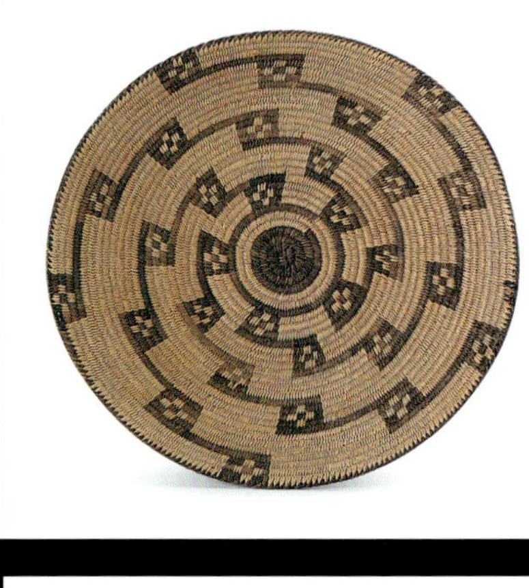
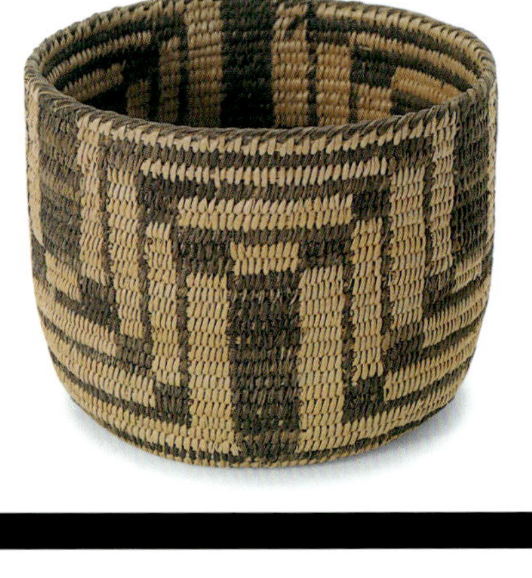
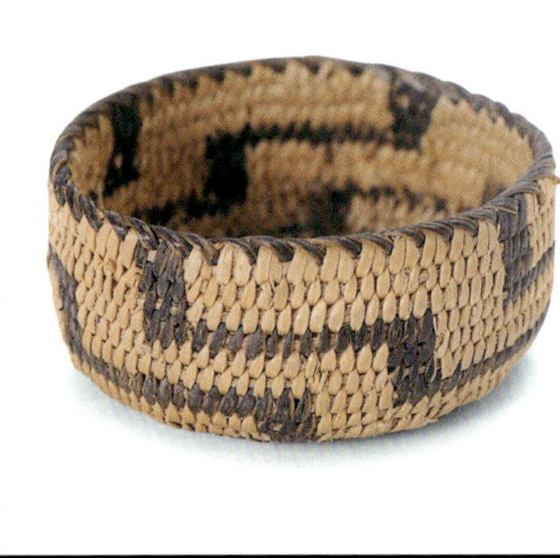
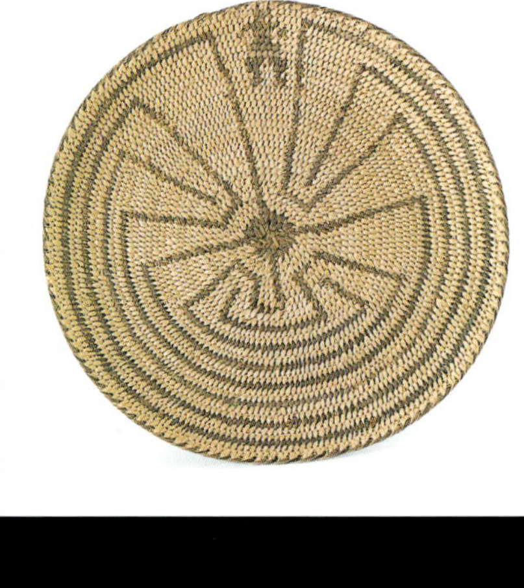
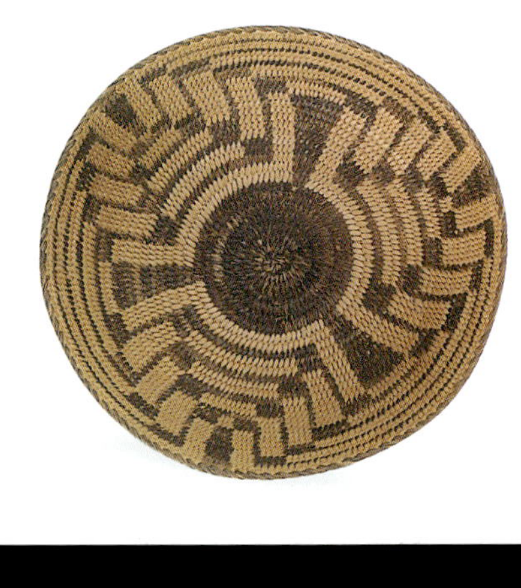

**TOP: AKIMEL O'ODHAM, 1920-1940s**
A woman gathers saguaro fruit. The fruit is picked out with red dyed willow and appears on the lid design as well.
1.25 x 1.25; 11 coils/inch, 28 stitches/inch. Close coiled on a cattail bundle with willow background and design sewn in devil's claw with red-dyed willow. Gift of the Henry Horner Straus Memorial, 3401-112A,B.

**BOTTOM: SUSIE WHITE, HIA CED O'ODHAM, 1920-1940**
.625 x 1; 24 coils/inch, 32 stitches/inch. Close coiled on a cattail bundle foundation with willow and devil's claw. Attributed to Susie White by weaver Rikki Francisco based on the evenness of the coils and the cleanly executed design on both the inside and outside of the basket. Purchased by Maie Heard for the original museum collection, NA-SW-PI-B-109.

**TOP: AKIMEL O'ODHAM, EARLY 1900s**
Quality, balance of design and a beautiful edge finish are typical of Pima work. The design is coyote tracks in a whirlwind, with the tracks shown in a negative design.
1 x 7.5; 8 coils/inch, 24 stitches/inch. Close coiled on a cattail bundle with willow and devil's claw sewing elements. Purchased by Maie Heard for the original museum collection, NA-SW-PI-B-12.

**BOTTOM: AKIMEL O'ODHAM, 1920s-1940s**
.0625 x 3.5; 24 coils/inch, 24 stitches/inch. Close coiled on a cattail bundle foundation with willow and devil's claw. Purchased by Maie Heard for the original museum collection, NA-SW-PI-B-42.

**TOP: SUSIE WHITE, HIA CED O'ODHAM, 1920-1940**
2 x 2.5; 12 coils/inch, 32 stitches/inch. Close coiled on a cattail bundle foundation with willow and devil's claw. Attributed to Susie White by weaver Rikki Francisco based on the evenness of the coils and the cleanly executed design on both the inside and outside of the basket. Purchased by Maie Heard for the original museum collection, NA-SW-PI-B-31.

**BOTTOM: AKIMEL O'ODHAM, 1920s-1940s**
.875 x 2.75; 16 coils/inch, 32 stitches/inch. Close coiled on a cattail bundle foundation with willow and devil's claw. Purchased by Maie Heard for the original museum collection, NA-SW-PI-B-104.

approached it with some pieces in mind. He had listened to commentary about the collection from weavers he had brought to the museum over the past several years. This was his first chance to consider the entire collection. Folwell was viewing the collection for the first time, and she shared the experience with her two daughters, Susan and Polly Rose, who are also potters continuing the tradition of ceramic innovation in another generation.

At an initial meeting, both Johnson and Jody Folwell resisted the idea of defining a masterwork in advance of viewing the collection. They wanted to have the experience of selecting pieces that spoke to them, deriving a message about masterworks from the pieces as they made selections. Their limits were the limits of the museum collection. As is often the case with museum collections, the Heard does not have the depth of contemporary pieces that would be ideal, especially with baskets, where its strengths lie with the great weaving traditions of the late 19th and early 20th centuries in the West. Many of the pieces in the collection are the art baskets of the period that attracted collectors, rather than the utilitarian baskets that a systematic anthropological approach to field collecting would have prescribed.

During the course of several separate sessions with the collection, some common approaches emerged. Both artists disregarded any time-based approach to the concept of masterworks. The bias of revering older pieces as coming from a more "traditional" or "unspoiled" time, and so being more authentic, was not remotely a consideration. And yet, both artists were very aware of the context within which a piece was produced and were intrigued by changes that have occurred. For example, Johnson was very impressed with the detailed design work that was done on the bases of some baskets. He remarked that such detailed work might not be done today on a basket made for sale that the weaver knew would sit on a shelf in a display case. The old baskets were made for use and were seen from all angles, by informed viewers who often knew the weaver.

Both artists treated the ceramics and baskets with the reverence that comes from an artist's understanding of the sacrifice and effort that the maker puts into a piece. Both artists spoke to the pieces as if each was a presence imbued with a spirit, an attitude that is shared by most of the Native advisors and artists who work with museum collections. Because they make similar pieces or have lived with people who do, they look at an artwork and see an artist. They visualize the creative process—the special effort the maker took, the difficult aspects, the mistakes. All of those thoughts came out as they explored and talked their way through pieces in the collection. For too many of these anonymous pieces, it is as close as we will come to learning from the person who created a masterpiece.

Early in the process, Folwell began to consider groupings of ceramics, bringing together pieces from many different traditions and time periods, making a kind of composed artwork from the individual pieces. She looked for the visual and intellectual relationships among pieces. Johnson, too, developed groupings that spoke less of the aesthetic relationships among basketry masterworks and more of the common ground weavers from different traditions shared. For example, one grouping presented masterful depictions of the weavers' environments, another, hidden details.

At the conclusion of the selection process, the guest curators joined by Folwell's daughter Susan spent a few minutes considering the experience. Jody Folwell commented that she "wanted everyone to see what our people have produced." Both guest curators had weighted their selections with pieces from traditions they understood best. For both artists, the process rejuvenated and inspired their own creative interests. Johnson remarked that the many projects of the Tohono O'odham Community Action program and preparations for the Celebration of Basketweaving Conference and Festival, to name a few of the activities he is involved in, can leave too little time for soul-restoring, creative work.

Change was another topic the two discussed. Both basketry and pottery are cultural arts in which change has been slow, as well as socially and economically risky. Both Folwell and Johnson are proponents of change while respecting tradition. Folwell commented that "tradition is the start of the process, and you move on from there." Susan Folwell said the potters have expressed to her their gratitude for her mother's innovative work, which freed them to experiment. She remarked, "Once freedom is set in place, it is like a bird let out of a cage."

Made by a male weaver who produces innovative pieces, Johnson's work has been controversial. He felt fortunate to have had the support of women teachers who felt that change was good. He recalled the support he received from his O'odham-speaking grandparents. For months, they accompanied him to basket lessons to act as translators for him as he was instructed by an O'odham-speaking teacher. On a lighter note, Johnson has also seen change in process. He told of two weavers who visit shopping malls where beargrass and yucca are used as decorative plants in the parking lot. There, they engage in some judicious "urban harvesting" or pruning. He talked about weavers who keep their hard-won basket materials in the refrigerator so they will not spoil and who use the flame of a lighter to clean stray fibers from a completed basket.

The final result of the process for each curator is very personal. In ceramics, Jody Folwell knows very well the technical challenges a potter faces working with plain, carved and polished ceramics. She knows the social environment of support and constraint that is the context for pueblo ceramics. Fortunately, potters today are receiving wider recognition and appreciation including public admiration of innovative ideas. In addition, they are also experiencing the financial rewards that come with appreciation to a much greater extent than basketweavers.

As an O'odham person, Johnson views baskets through the personal lens of his own experience, knowing both the rewards and struggles of weaving. It might surprise some to know that a part of the information presented at the annual basket conference that Johnson organizes is information that deals with the weavers' health. The production of a basket can lead to health problems, as a weaver works with wet materials in a very repetitive motion, body twist-

ed to achieve just the right angle to maintain pressure and tension on the basket. He understands the role basketweavers can play in their communities, teaching and reviving cultural traditions among young people. He knows the economic potential of baskets to provide income to people seeking to live a more traditional lifestyle. At present, the potential does not equal that of pottery making, but the hope is that there will be improvement and that weavers will find sufficient rewards of a personal and cultural nature to continue weaving.

Being Native in America can mean making difficult choices about the extent to which one participates in Native culture and cultural arts. These guest curators have brought new voices that enrich our understanding and appreciation of the Native artistic traditions. The baskets and ceramics in the Heard collection spoke across cultures; the guest curators listened and could hear them. This—told to you in the pages that follow in their own words—is what they heard.

Dr. Ann E. Marshall is Director of Collections, Education and Interpretation at the Heard Museum.

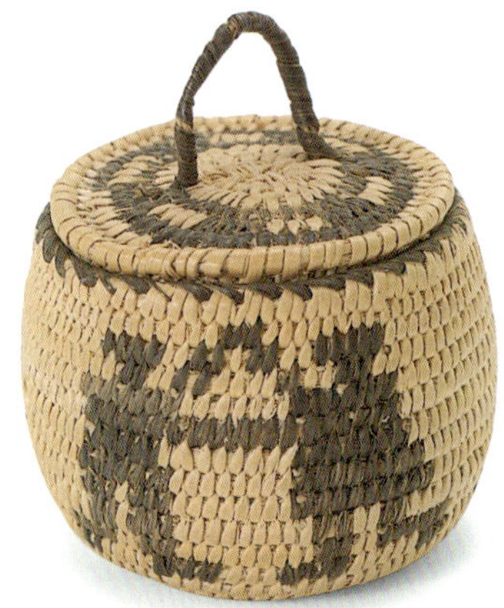

**AKIMEL O'ODHAM MINIATURE BASKET, 1920s-1940s**
1.52 x 1.25; 16 coils/inch, 24 stitches/inch. Close coiled on a cattail bundle foundation with willow and devil's claw. Purchased by Maie Heard for the original museum collection, NA-SW-PI-B-153.

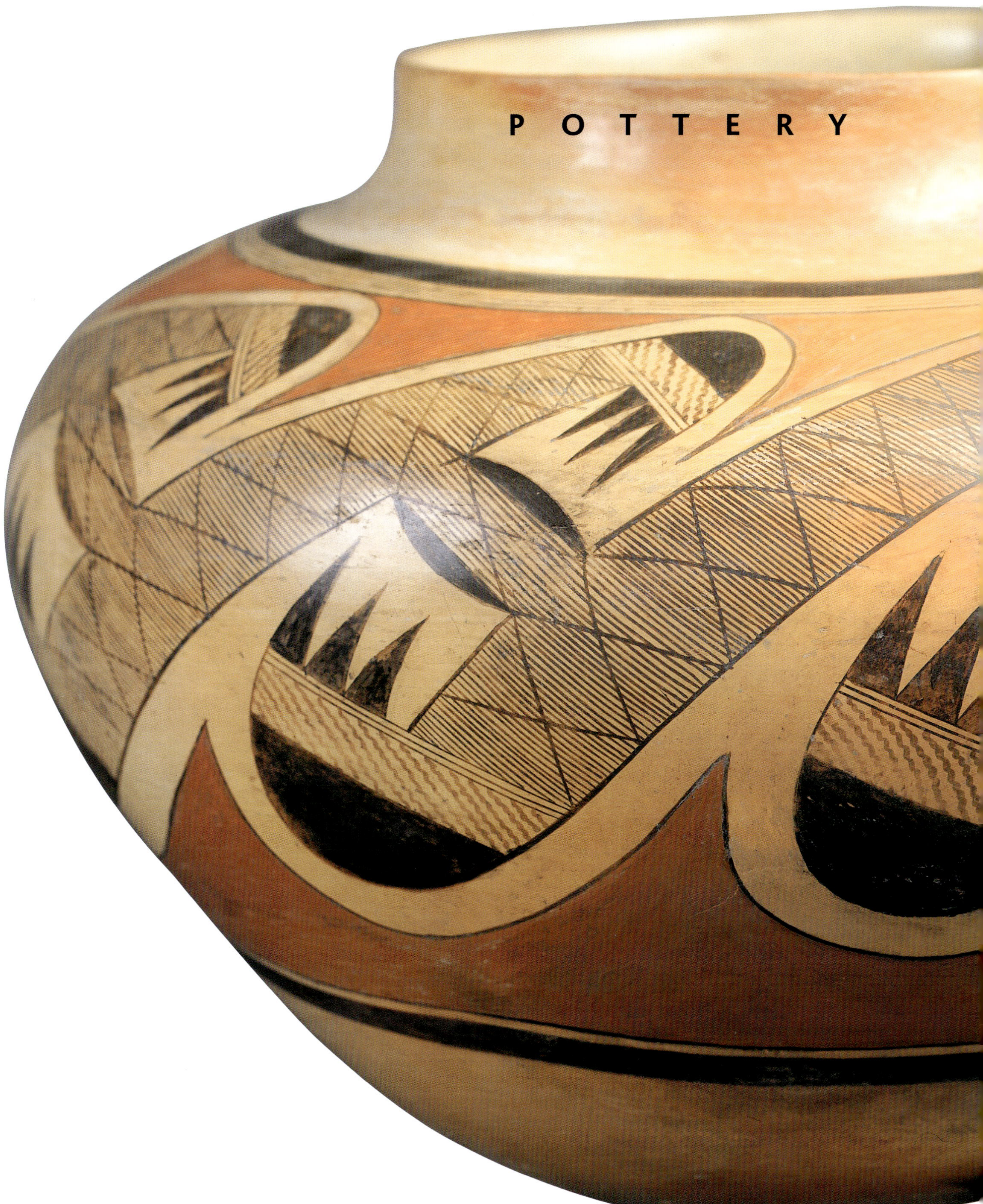
POTTERY

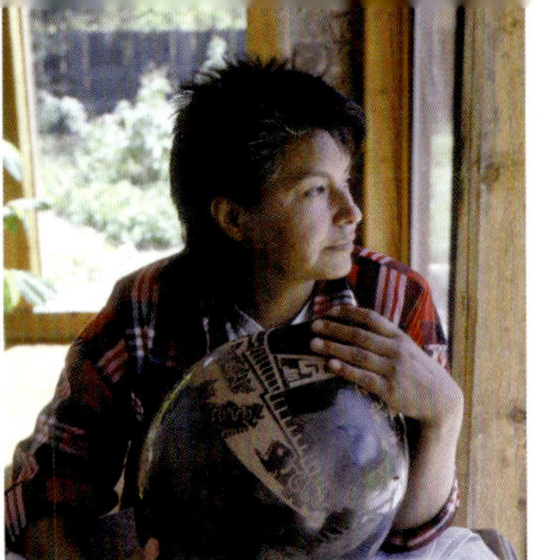



# POTTERY

## THEME AND VARIATION

### BY JODY FOLWELL AND DIZA SAUERS

TO FULLY UNDERSTAND the nature of pueblo pottery, one must grasp the fact that pottery is an extension and reflection of the evolution of a people. As pueblo culture has continued to embrace its moment in time, honor traditions and forge new ways of being, our pottery has experienced similar transformations. It is possible to witness how the passage of time has molded and altered not only the role of pottery, but also the symbiotic relationship pottery plays in preserving a way of being.

Throughout history, pottery adopted the shape of basic functional form. One can trace the evolution of pottery from its most historical utilitarian functions to its most current incarnation on the cutting edge, as artists question their own traditions. In a singular fashion, pottery provides an ongoing documentation of the advancement of time and its influence on a people and their survival.

Because the pots gathered here represent a far-reaching scope in time—spanning at least 200 years—the way we study their growth and development is important. Still more pressing is to note the way these pots speak to one another, forming and informing one another despite the hundreds of years that have passed between them. These pots provide us with a striking sense of continuity and community, ways of remembering and seeing, a tangible definition of our own history and current moment.

The selections explore the dynamics of how pottery transcends time. One cannot truly explain why some connections are so vibrant and electric, why some pieces leap up and resonate with one another. In some mysterious fashion, certain pots seem to effortlessly complete a thought that started hundreds of years before. The very way these pots interact becomes a way of seeing, a lens for understanding the unity found amongst pueblo potters as a people and as artists.

A true artist in the process of creation does not set out to purposely design a masterwork. The artist sets out to join the ancient tradition of finding and recording beauty.

If beauty is in the eye of the beholder, then it is the individual viewer who defines what is a masterwork. Where one finds beauty is a result of a lifelong activity of assembling an aesthetic. For some, beauty is based on harmony. For others, dissonance. For some, it is a sense of endurance or a sense of that which is beyond us. Often, beauty is identified by the viewer strictly as a personal statement. Perhaps one does not fully grasp or recognize the reason, but feels a spiritual connection, an arc of recognition that may come from a subconscious agreement of color, image, shape. Perhaps it is with a slight sigh of inner happiness, a silent gasp, an inner electrical flow, and the final rush of contentment, but we know. We receive the signal that we are in the presence of greatness. One knows when one is in the company of a masterwork when one forgets the self.

In some indefinable way, what one finds in these masterworks is the result of artists having transcended their own moments. Perhaps they poured a bit of themselves into the pot, an intangible sense of the self that speaks to the recipient. Perhaps the pot itself, now an artifact long separated from the hands that formed it, provides a way for us to speak to it, and maybe to listen, to think about all the hearts and hands that have held it. A masterwork is both a product and a part of time. A masterwork compels us both to listen and to speak; it is a talisman that lets us enter a small piece of history that we can join in the way that human beings were meant to—not with a sense of ownership, but with a sense of continuance, a sense of passage. These pots offer us a way of joining, for our own brief moment that we are here, and then of passing on. — **JODY FOLWELL, WITH POLLY FOLWELL, SUSAN FOLWELL AND DIZA SAUERS**

Diza Sauers, twice recipient of the Arizona Commission on the Arts Fellowship, teaches writing at the University of Arizona.

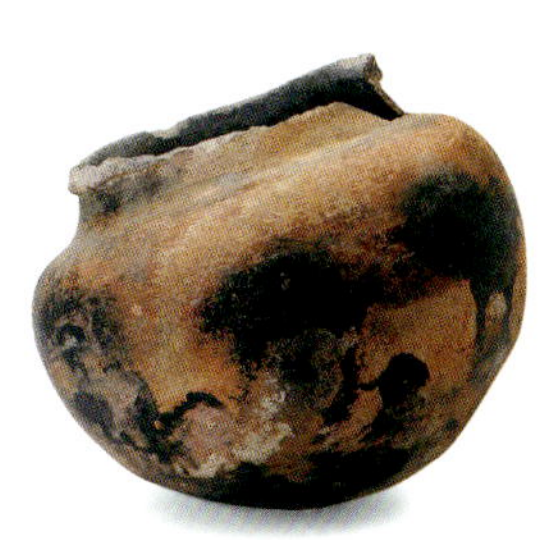
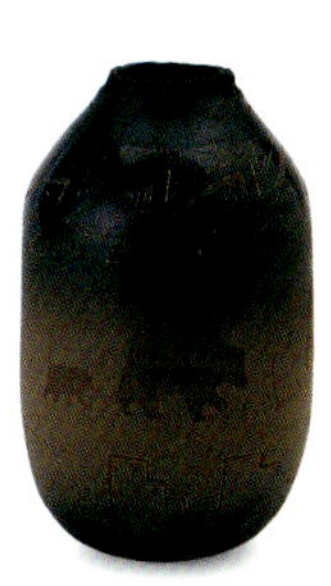
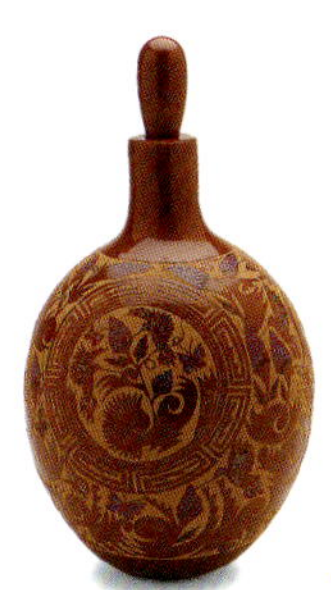
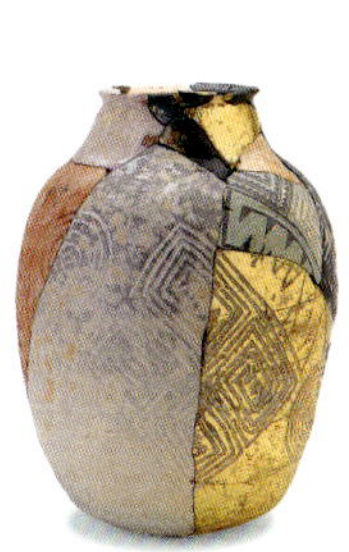
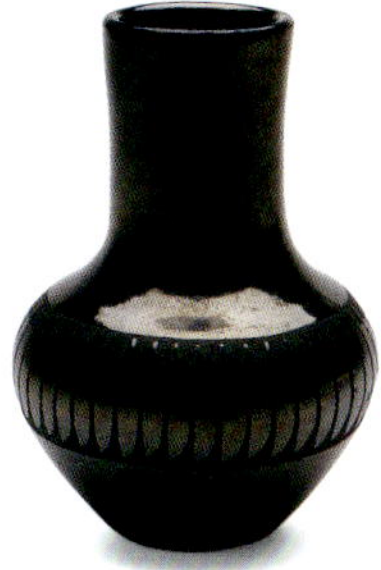

# Bridging Time

*Time has gracefully evolved this 19th-century Hopi cooking jar into a true masterpiece. Observe the coloration, shape and the crackled lip. This bowl has sustained life in elegance.*

**HOPI COOKING JAR,** 19th century

13 x 15.5. Heard Museum Purchase,
NA-SW-HO-A1-34.

P E R H A P S the most dramatic example of bridging time can be seen when viewing pieces by Polly Rose Folwell and Grace Medicine Flower alongside a Hopi cooking jar from the 1800s. One can swiftly trace the arc from accidental historical footnote to a modern acknowledgment of the medium's properties. The cracked earthen rims on two of the pots speak to one another directly, but with different intent. The Hopi jar acts as a signifier, a way of remembering. One hundred years later, the cracked rim on Folwell's bear pot indicates a fundamental shift in thinking about the nature and role of pottery. Embracing a high sense of aesthetics and the ability to acknowledge history through remembrance and evocation, the modern pieces provide an ironic twist. Yet we also see that aesthetics do not transcend the medium; in the most elemental way, they are the same. One hundred years later, they are still one.

---

Comments accompanying objects throughout the book are in the words of the guest curators.

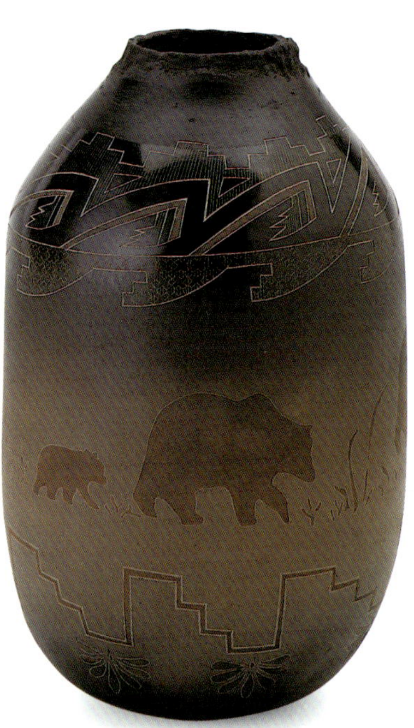

*Time travels from the 19th-century Hopi cooking vessel to the 2001 Polly Rose Folwell jar. Polly's rendition of the earthen cracks on the lip of her jar is history in the making. She is a true innovator of pueblo pottery.*

**POLLY ROSE FOLWELL**
Santa Clara, b. 1962
**Jar, 2001**

12 x 6.5. Heard Museum Purchase,
4108-1.

The way that some pieces travel side by side and complete one another is partly what distinguishes pueblo pottery as a tangent of community life. Looking at a jar by the venerated Maria Martinez (circa 1970) together with one by contemporary artist Nathan Begay (2000), we get an intimate glimpse of the tight dialogue between some pieces. Begay's awareness of his moment in time manifests itself in the fractured segmentation of his pot. The color and unorthodox materials place his work firmly in a post-modern era. Yet when his work sits next to the lyrical piece by Maria Martinez, one instantly sees between them an interplay in form, design and craftsmanship. While Begay's vessel remains within the constraints of traditional pottery by virtue of his use of pueblo-style imagery, he provides an interesting insight on the pause between generations, a slight breath in time.

*Grace Medicine Flower's delicate designs and movement of shape lend one to take a deep breath and sigh gently.*

**GRACE MEDICINE FLOWER**
Santa Clara, b. 1938
Jar with lid, 1991

13.5 x 6.75. Gift of John and Rita Rye, 4110-3A,B.

*Maria Martinez's perfectly polished, symmetrical shape and Santana Martinez's precise feather painting on the jar represent a Golden Age in pueblo pottery.*

**MARIA MARTINEZ AND SANTANA MARTINEZ**
San Ildefonso, 1890-1980 and b. 1909
Jar, c. 1970

9 x 6. Gift of Edward Jacobson, NA-SW-SI-A10-22.

*The silhouettes of time play a merriment of songs on the traditional designs of this contemporary vessel. A magical intertwining of traditional and contemporary concepts makes for a masterpiece.*

**NATHAN BEGAY**
Navajo
Jar, 2000

14.5 x 9. Purchased by the Heard Museum at the Heard Museum Shop, 4073-1.

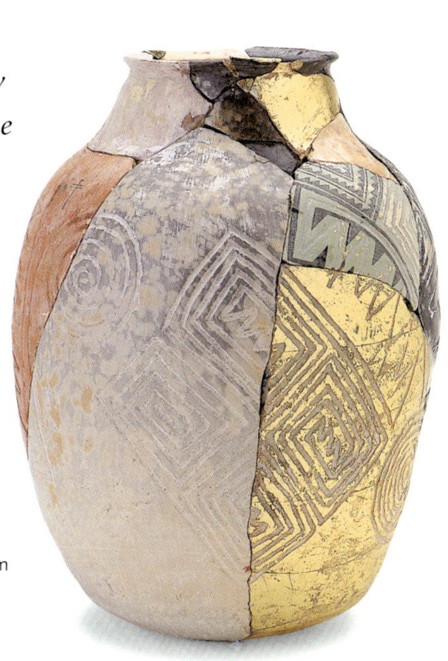

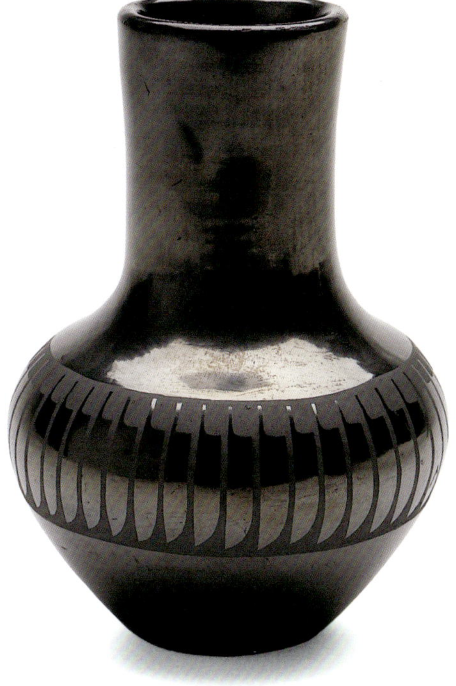

**I**NEVITABLY, one can trace the introduction of the world of commerce into pottery. Slowly, we witness the shift in awareness from the pot used as utensil into the pot as commodity. Despite the geographical and temporal distances represented in this grouping, a pivotal moment is captured. Here, we see pottery become aware of the idea of profit. The Acoma jar by Jessie Garcia, below right, was clearly made not only with tradition in mind, but also the intent to sell. The craftsmanship follows tradition but the design is ornate; the jar is not meant to be pressed into service but to appeal to a buyer. This shift marks a highly formalized sense of design, unlike the freedom and joy found in the Mexican olla, which reminds us that form for the sake of function granted artists a certain liberty and artistic license. These lashings of mineral colorings on the Mexican olla were used not simply as a sealant, but to make an aesthetic statement. The joyful design on this pot is reminiscent of Jackson Pollock, yet the random and unfettered lines were

ity. The delicacy of both line and form, as well as the ghostly aspect of the water serpent, permits this pot to also transcend its own moment in time and space. The San Juan and Blue Corn pots are centered simply and beautifully by Mark Tahbo's jar. Completing the variation on the theme, Tahbo's work is direct and powerful in its flow of image and design. The swift cycle captured on the surface of his work narrows the circle and closes in on a pure moment encapsulated, the swift center of a spinning wheel.

*"Clay touches you, it brings you in and grounds you."* Susan Folwell, 2001

# Commerce + Aesthetics

made to please no one but the artist. Nathan Youngblood's carefully crafted piece, shown at the top of the next page, has a beautifully executed sense of design firmly located in the present moment. While carefully built with a sense of unity and beautifully polished, it is also careful to please.

While pottery clearly begins to make a shift into straddling the worlds of finance and form, some works stay rooted in celebrating clay in a way that transcends time and enters the realm of universality. Three pots on the facing page speak of the power of clay to act as a transport. The large San Juan storage jar looks almost Asian in the two-tone burnishing. The simple, strong two-tone mineral coloring still extends itself, after a hundred years, well beyond its time period like Blue Corn's avanyu pot, which also provides a strikingly elegant design of Asian sensibil-

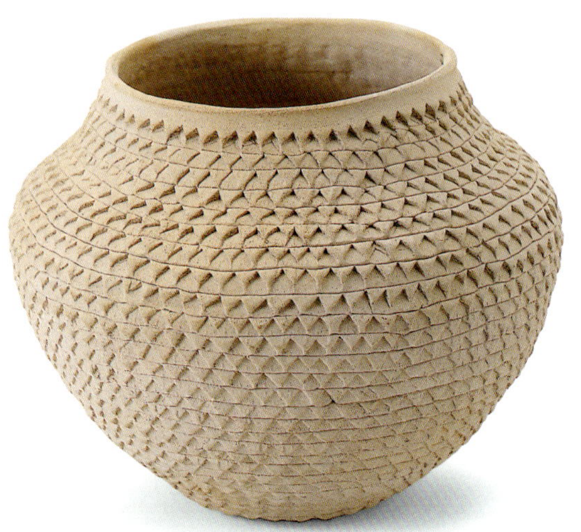

**JESSIE GARCIA**
**Acoma**
**Jar, 1966**
10.5 x 12. Purchased by the Heard Museum from Byron Hunter's Trading Post, Phoenix, Arizona, NA-SW-AC-A8-1.

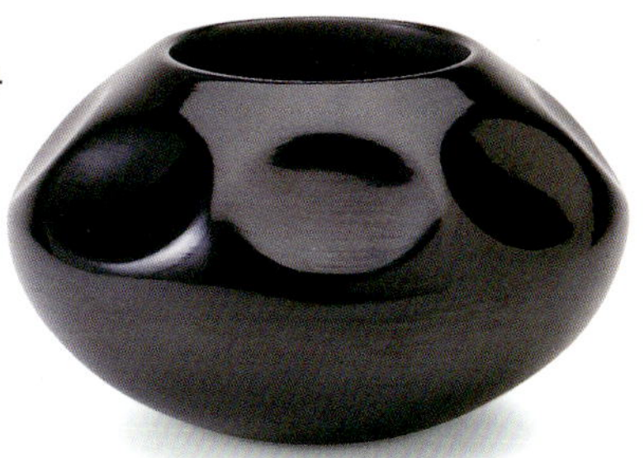

**NATHAN YOUNGBLOOD**
**Santa Clara, b. 1954**
**Jar, 1991**

5 x 8. Purchased by the Heard Museum from Gallery 10, Scottsdale, Arizona, NA-SW-SC-A10-70.

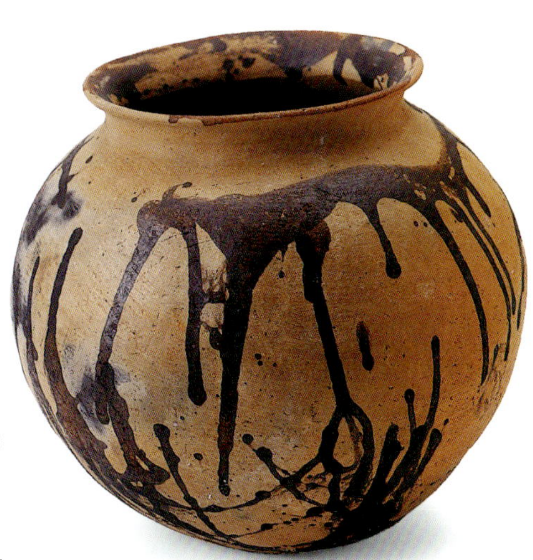

**MEXICAN OLLA, 1979**

11.5 x 12. Acquired for the Heard Museum from the village of Santo Domingo Tonaltepec, Oaxaca, by the Museo Nacional de Artes. Heard Museum Purchase, NA-MX-MX-A12-5.

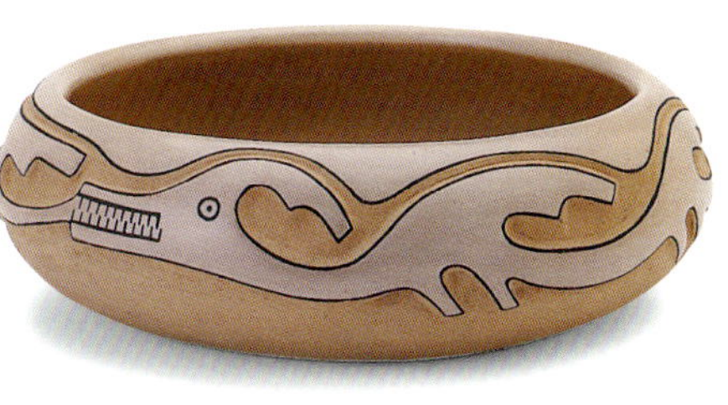

**BLUE CORN**
**San Ildefonso, 1922-1999**
**Bowl, c. 1967**

3.75 x 12. Gift of Richard F. Chedester, NA-SW-SI-A7-13.

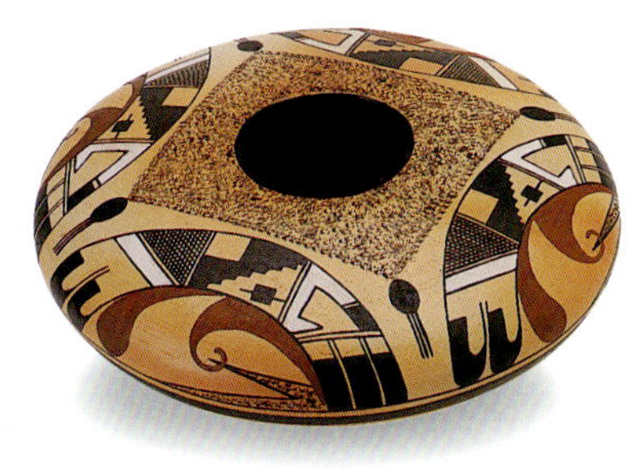

**MARK TAHBO**
**Hopi-Tewa, b. 1958**
**Jar, 1991**

3.5 x 7.5. Purchased by the Heard Museum from the artist, NA-SW-HO-A7-179.

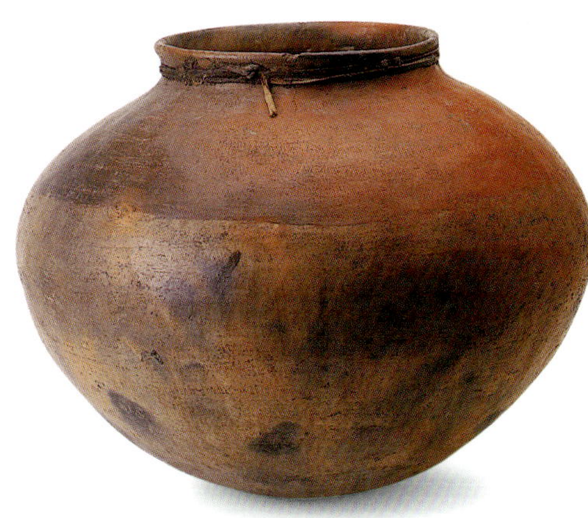

**SAN JUAN STORAGE JAR, c. 1900**

17.5 x 23. Fred Harvey Fine Arts Collection, 145P.

*The Mexican olla extends beyond its region. With a touch of paint splashes, the artist gives an indication of a need for experimentation and innovation.*

*Nathan Youngblood learned to make pottery from his grandmother, Margaret Tafoya. She would tell him, "take a little time especially with polishing and you will be rewarded." Youngblood is one of the most venerated and accomplished potters of the 20th century. The shape, architectural form, polishing and firing make his jar a masterwork.*

*The stark white avanyu on the surface of Blue Corn's bowl is an unusual approach to creating a pueblo traditional design, suggesting a need for a bit of experimentation.*

*Mark Tahbo's pot is perfection in aesthetics. A jewel. It is a technically beautiful pot.*

*We are drawn to the old, searching and seeking for stability, strength and beauty that the object may possess.*

# Concept + Design

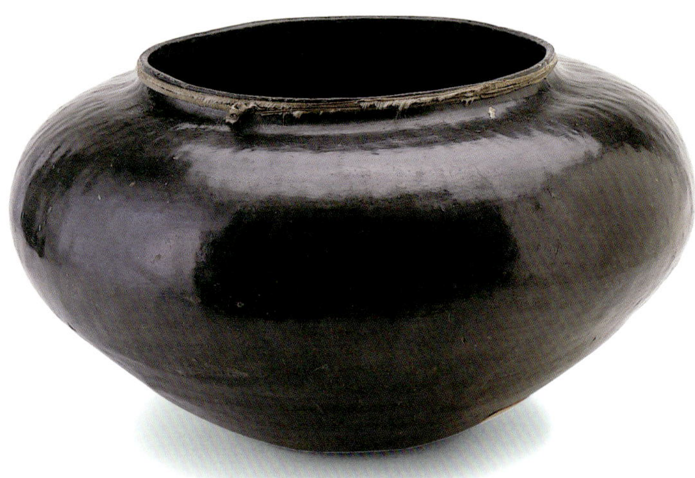

**SARA FINA**
**Santa Clara, c. 1863-1949**
**Bowl, early 1900s**

13 x 23. Identified by Margaret Tafoya in 1994 as the work of her mother, Sara Fina. Fred Harvey Fine Arts Collection, 599P.

*This is a phenomenal piece. Looking at some distinguishing features, we find that prior to 1950, potters did not have sandpaper. Consequently, Sara Fina probably used a volcanic stone or corn cob to sand the unfired bowl. The bowl also has another distinguishing feature—it is polished on the inside, which is a very difficult task to accomplish.*

*When pots are large, potters use big strokes when polishing and often push hard, which leaves impressions in the surfaces of the clay. This pottery was polished softly with a light touch. Margaret Tafoya had a special talent for polishing.*

T HE UNITY in the grouping of two large Santa Clara pots and a Diego Romero bowl derives from the wide range found in the solid possibility of clay. A lovely study in lineage can be traced in the two pots by mother and daughter. Both Sara Fina's pot and her daughter Margaret Tafoya's piece use large voluminous shapes to ponder the solid nature of clay. Both pieces give evidence of work rising from a time of careful crafting, as these pots are meticulously polished both inside and out.

**MARGARET TAFOYA**
**Santa Clara, 1904-2001**
**Jar, 1925**

23 x 19.5. Identified by Margaret Tafoya in 1994 as a jar she made in 1925 and sold in Santa Fe, New Mexico. Fred Harvey Fine Arts Collection, 603P.

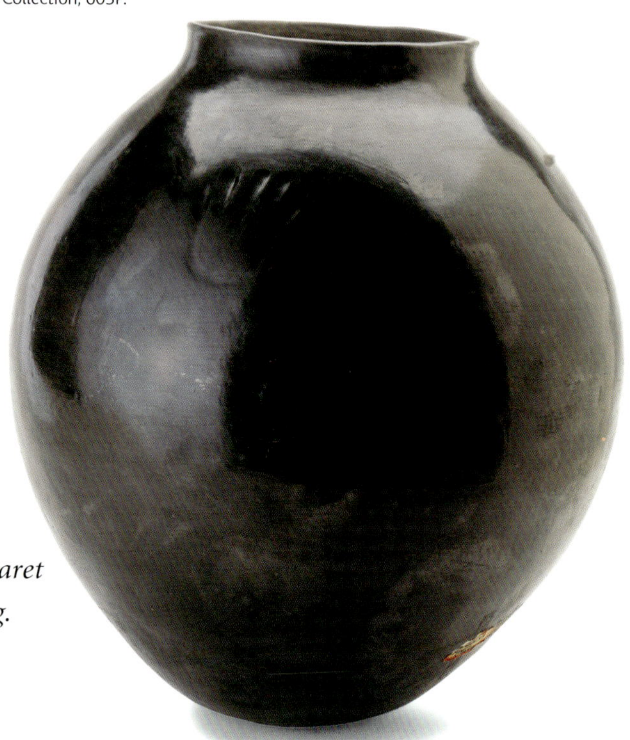

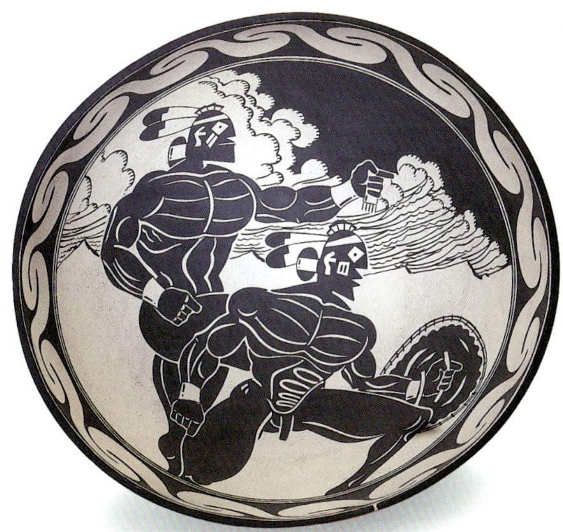

**DIEGO ROMERO**
Cochiti, b. 1964
**Bowl, 2000**

6.75 x 12. Purchased by the Heard Museum from Faust Gallery,
Scottsdale, Arizona, 4038-1.

*Diego Romero's innovative Mimbres-style bowl is a new approach to an artistic expression. He is a true artist, applying high technical skill with great creativity.*

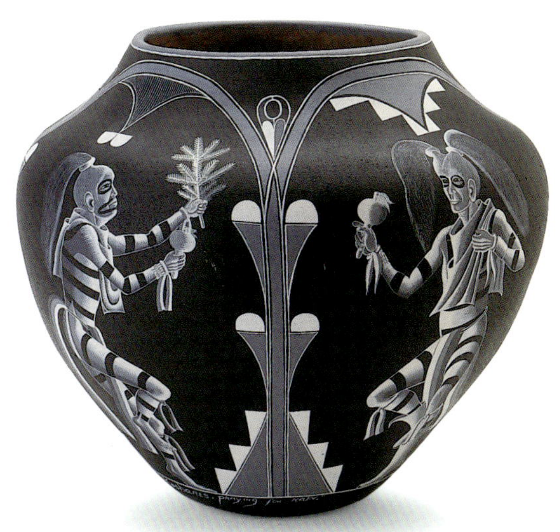

**RAFAEL AND SOFIA P. MEDINA**
Zia, b. 1932 and b. 1929
**Jar, 1972**

11.75 x 12.75. Acquired by the donors at the Heard Museum Shop. Gift from
the Estate of Herman and Claire Blum, 3576-134.

*The Koshare pot is electrifying. It is reminiscent of a feast day in August when the clowns are pulling out the spirits from the earth, making unworldly sounds.*

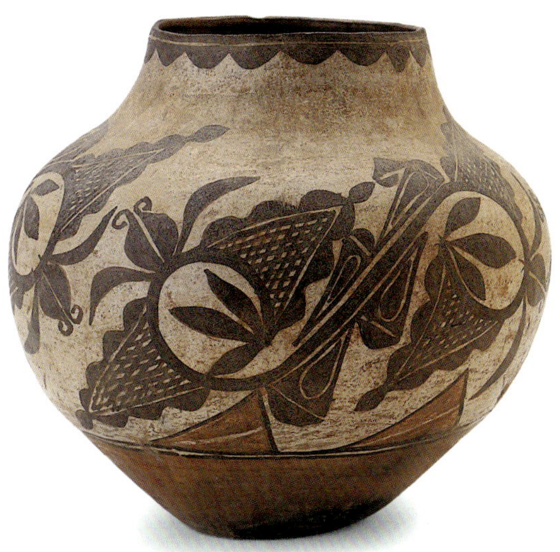

**ZIA WATER JAR, LATE 1800s**

10.75 x 11.75. Fred Harvey Fine Arts Collection, 263P.

*This is a wonderful classical jar representing balance and elegance. The whole composition of the jar including structure, polishing and painting is strong and subtle. This is a highly technical piece of artwork.*

The outstanding technique of Sara Fina and Tafoya's pots provides a sound and wonderful counterpart to the levity and power found in Diego Romero's modern tableau. Reminiscent of the Mimbres work in both design and concept, Romero's modern depictions of life are portrayed using an ancient technique: the pictorial narrative. Whether these human figures are captured hunting, fishing, mating or planting, Romero underscores the fact that the most pressing moments in life are lived now as they have been for thousands of years. These human moments of revelation, captured in clay, speak to one another about survival, adaptability and the very essence of humanity.

As a unit, the Rafael and Sofia P. Medina pot and Zia water jar, shown on the preceding page, thunder together to complete one another in ways that are electric and completely unexpected. In the same way that any ceremony relies on the unity of its pieces—the singers and dancers and audience all coming together—the disparate elements of these pots rush together and fuse to complete one another only in the presence of the other. The imagery in the Medinas' pot is ceremonial in nature, indicative of tradi-

tion, yet their use of non-traditional materials, the shocking, almost neon aspect of the white and the black in the paints, is insistently contemporary. Further, the images are never merely two-dimensional figures but take on dimension and depth in a thoroughly modern fashion. When it is placed next to the Zia water jar from the early 1900s, an unexpected resonance occurs. The water jar is classic, basic in both design and its soft, muted earth tones. These same soft flesh tones are subtly employed in the Medina pot to capture the rhythm and the understated hue in the three-dimensional edges of the clowns and dancers. No matter what pueblo, there is a unity that binds all potters, an unspoken acknowledgement that we all come from the same place of origin; this strong sense of belonging is found in the way these two pots effortlessly complete one another.

In some instances, history points out to us patterns marked into clay that speak of human limitation. This group of three parrot pots (separated by more than a hundred years) centers itself around the image of the bird. The parrot's historical context, however, changes over time, speaking clearly about



**TAMMY GARCIA**
**Santa Clara, b. 1969**
**Jar, 1995**

13.5 x 12. Purchased by the Heard Museum from Gallery 10, Scottsdale, Arizona, 3557-1.

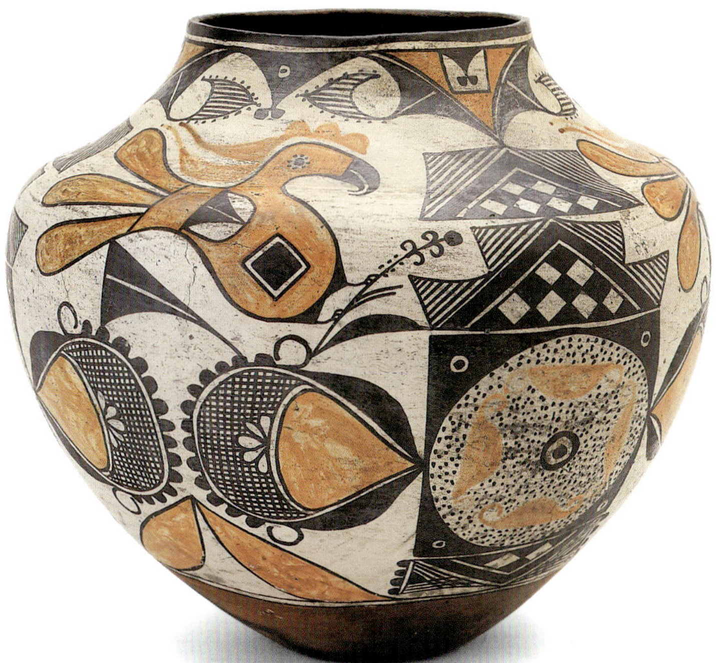

**ACOMA JAR, c. 1890**

12 x 12. Fred Harvey Fine Arts Collection, 508P.

*This is one of the most important examples and shows the similarities, contrasts and interplay of designs among pueblo potters. This jar, along with the Zia canteen and the jar by Tammy Garcia, all form the cycle of eternal life among the pueblos.*

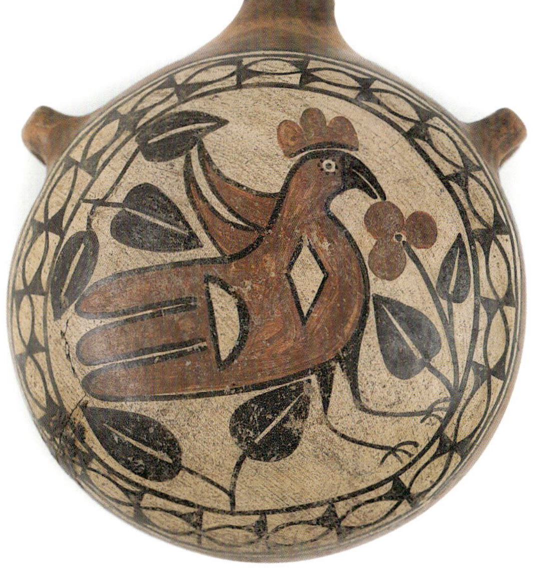

**ZIA CANTEEN, 1875-1900**

5 x 8.5 x 8. Acquired by the Harvey Company in the early 1900s from Frederick Volz, a trader at Canyon Diablo, Arizona. Fred Harvey Fine Arts Collection, 85P.

*Drink to contentment with this late 1800s water canteen.*

the rapid transition between function and form. The Zia water canteen appears to be ceremonial in nature, with a complex design and centered figure that suggest ritual use. The Acoma storage vessel is utilitarian, and its painted birds were probably meant simply to please the eye. By the time we arrive in the latter half of the 20th century, the bird has become entrapped in consumer expectation; it is readily identifiable, easily reproduced and, therefore, desirable. When work becomes merely decorative

and dictated by the consumer, an imposed set of expectations constricts and confines the artist. We are left to wonder how pottery can continue to evolve when artists become firmly lodged and limited inside consumer expectations, as opposed to fulfilling their own expressions of self.

D ESPITE the difficulty of working inside the constraints of consumer demands, pueblo pottery continues to evolve and define itself. Contemporary potters emerge, as they always have, to take the medium a step further, to challenge boundaries, to enter the spiral as it circles back around, and moves up and out. The pottery pictured here begins to define new boundaries. The twist on traditional roles is echoed in Richard Zane Smith's pot, in which exposed coils and design honor traditional methods commonly found in basketry. The color and textures, the spiraling pattern, the nod to the ancient origin of pottery through a texture similar to weaving—all challenge the very boundaries of clay and, consequently, form. This forward step is taken even further by Susan Folwell's Harry Potter bowl, which provides wry commentary on the

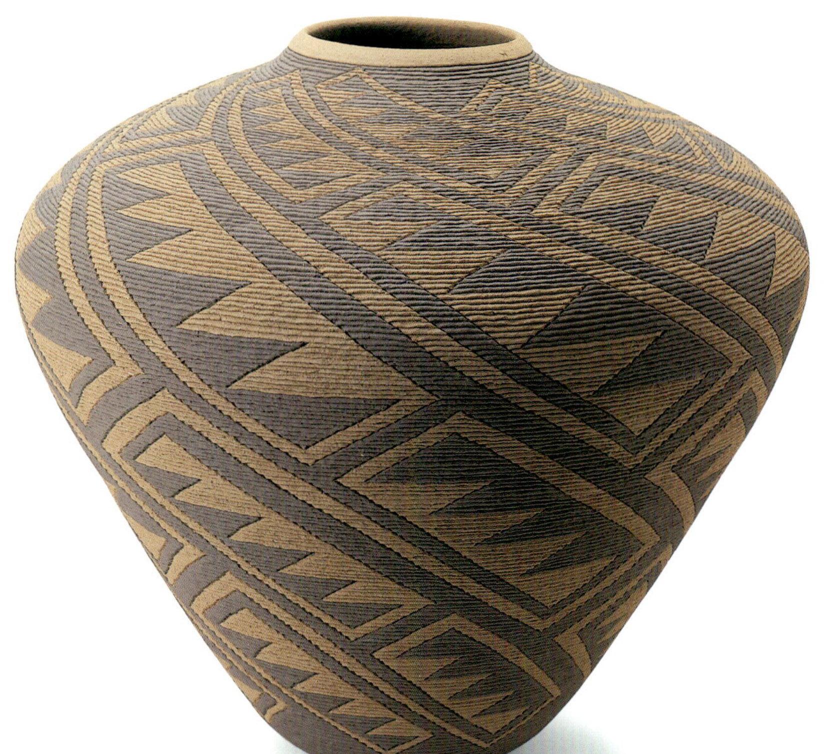


*This bowl illustrates singular boldness and intuitive creativity.*

**SUSAN FOLWELL**
**Santa Clara, b. 1970**
**Bowl, 2001**

2.5 x 11.5. Heard Museum Purchase, 4109-1.

aesthetics of consumption by questioning a mass-marketed sense of contemporary mythology. Provoking social commentary and resting on the pinnacle of the idea of art for art's sake, her work defies the consumer's relentless desire for "traditional Native imagery" by commenting on the very need for mass consumption. Suspended on the image of the spiral, her images float her work up and out of a traditional realm to rest firmly on the cutting edge of contemporary Native work.

**RICHARD ZANE SMITH**
**Wyandot, b. 1955**
**Jar, 1986**

17.5 x 20. Acquired by the donors at Gallery 10, Scottsdale, Arizona. Gift from the Family of Adrienne and Jerome Harold Kay, 3827-6.

*There is an outstanding skill, beauty and ease in all of Richard Zane Smith's pottery—the geometrical design flows and gives way to a rhythmic movement. Observe the use of the light pastel colors, which brings out the softness of the rough texture.*

*A soft, gentle breeze blew through the ruins of a window and quietly landed on a white fragile bowl, speaking of a time past. This pot speaks volumes of the technical skills, polishing and creativity involved in forming an artistic piece.*

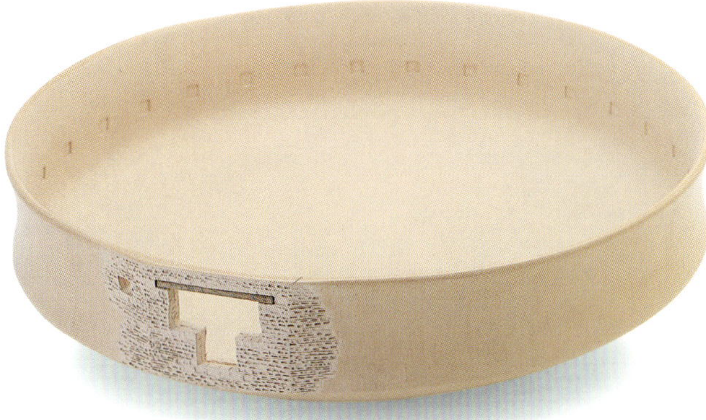

**AL QÖYAWAYMA**
**Hopi, b. 1938**
**Bowl, 1988**

5.5 x 16.375. Acquired at Gallery 10, Scottsdale, Arizona. Anonymous Donor, 4012-1.

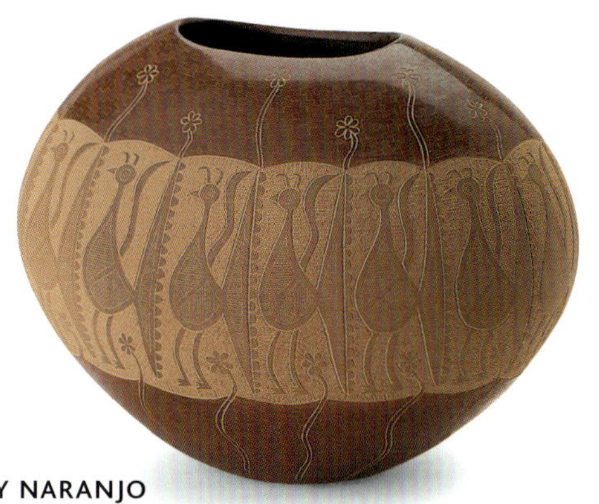

**JODY NARANJO**
**Santa Clara, b. 1969**
**Bowl, 1999**

10 x 12 x 7.5. Purchased by the Heard Museum with funds donated by Mr. and Mrs. H. James Douglass from the 41st Annual Heard Museum Guild Indian Fair & Market, where it received a best of division award, 3850-1.

*Give me a song to sing by. The exquisitely oval-shaped bowl works perfectly with the elongated sand crane motif. The main design is enhanced by the use of an intricate lace background.*

To understand our history is to understand ourselves. The interrelationships among these pieces provide a way of glimpsing not only the evolution of an ancient art form, but to witness the moment of emergence as we begin to break into new territory and claim new ground. To stand in the presence of these pots and consider their varying moments in history forces the eye to behold not only the remarkable capacity of clay to suspend time, but also to provide testimony about the evolution of pottery, from its utilitarian role to one consciously concerned with preservation, aesthetics and progress. In a deep way, these groupings clearly teach us not only about how time marks itself, but how a cycle of life is sustained, marked and remembered in the pottery world.

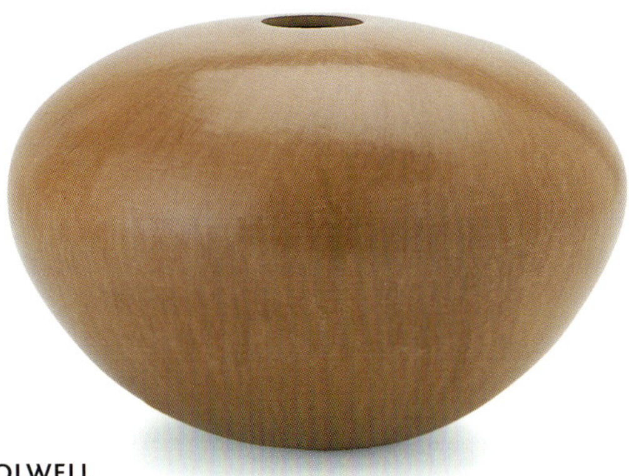

**JODY FOLWELL**
**Santa Clara, b. 1942**
**Jar, 1978**

7.5 x 11. Purchased by the Heard Museum from the 1978 Heard Museum Guild Arts & Crafts Exhibit, NA-SW-SC-A1-12.

# Evolution + Definition

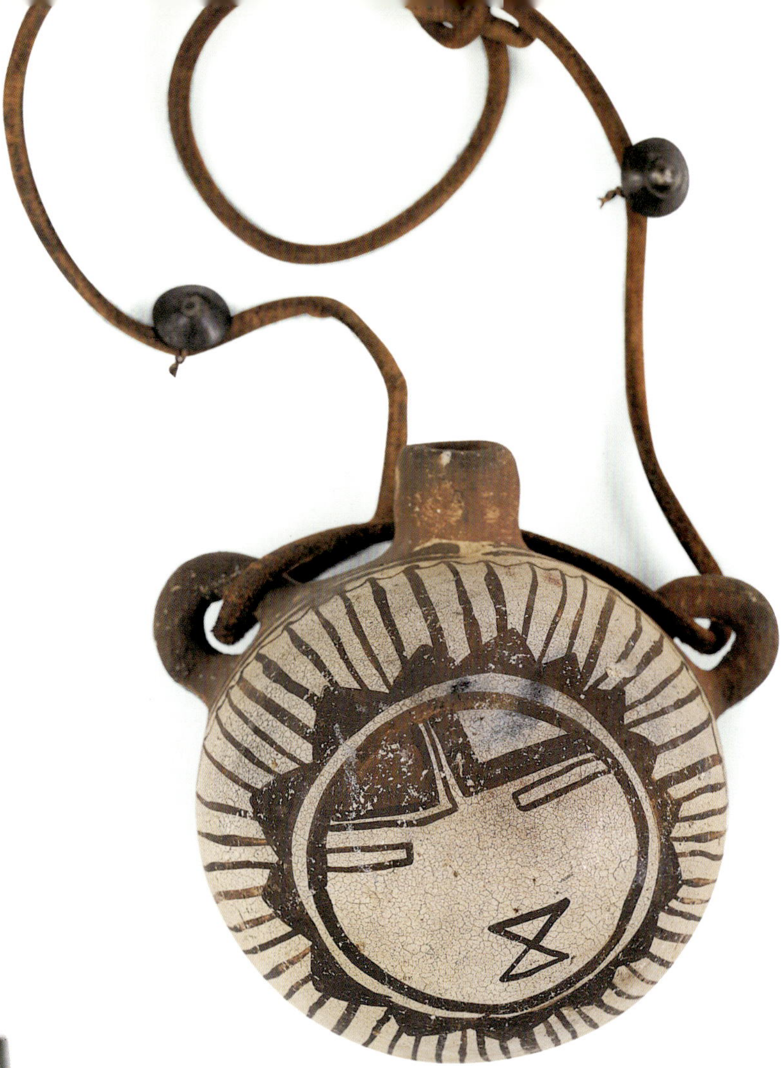

*Rose Gonzales created a strong and simple avanyu design, although during the firing the avanyu took on a life by adorning itself with a metallic sheen.*

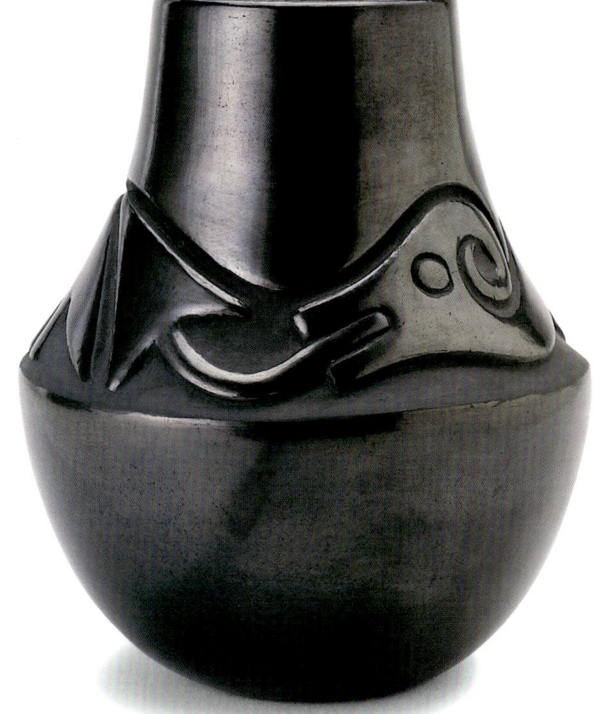

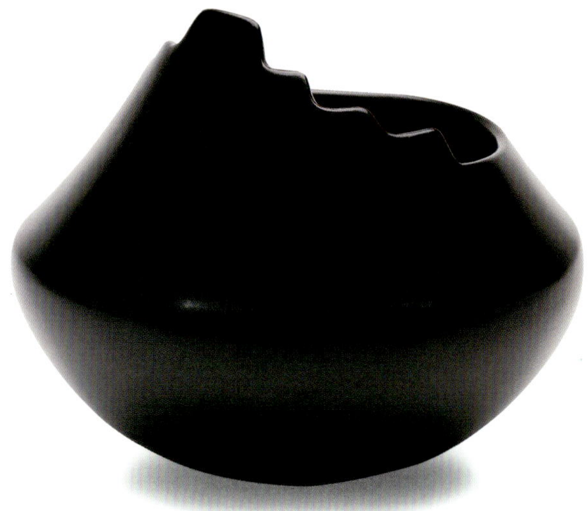

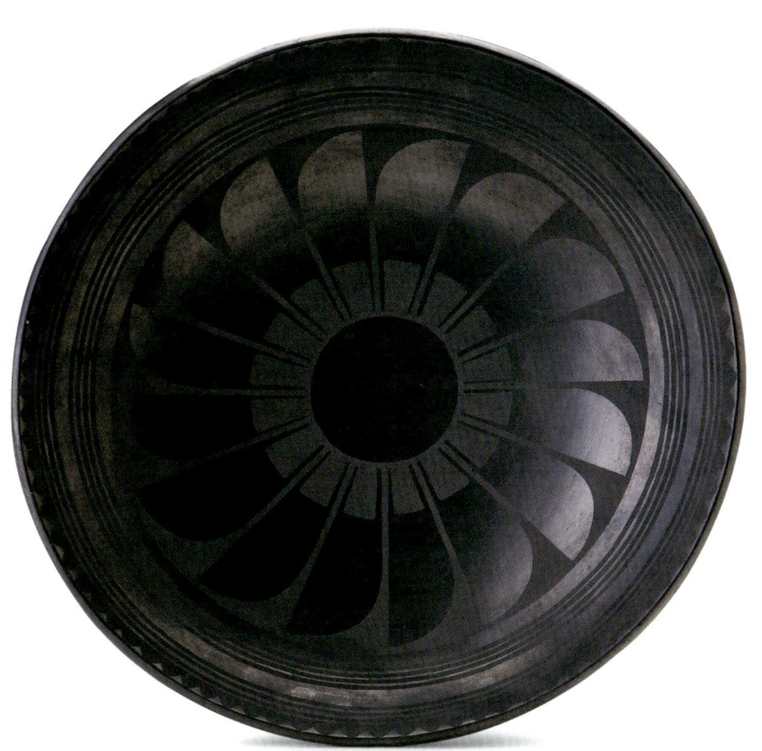

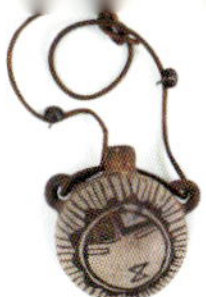

**HOPI CANTEEN, LATE 1800s**
4 x 4.5 x 5. Gift of Mr. David Treat, NA-SW-HO-A7-79.

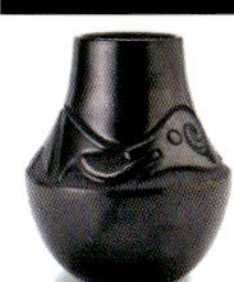

**ROSE GONZALES**
San Juan, 1900-1989
Jar, c. 1965
9.5 x 7.5. Gift of Edward Jacobson, NA-SW-SI-A10-54.

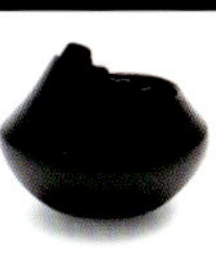

**TINA GARCIA**
Santa Clara, b. 1957
Jar, 1988
7.5 x 7.5. Acquired by the donor at the Andrews Gallery in Albuquerque, New Mexico. Given in memory of Dr. Stuart G. Meibuhr, 4099-2.

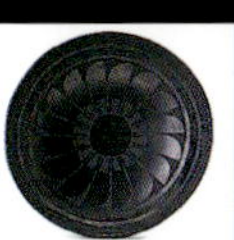

**MARIA AND JULIAN MARTINEZ**
San Ildefonso, 1890-1980 and 1897-1943
Plate, 1925-1943
3 x 14. Gift of Madeline and Russell Warren, 3465-1.

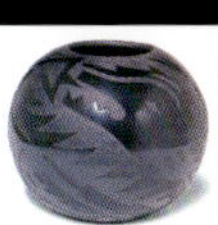

**JOSEPH LONEWOLF**
Santa Clara, b. 1932
Jar, 1970
4 x 5.5. Gift of Edward Jacobson, NA-SW-SC-A10-35.

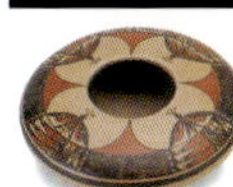

**DEXTRA QUOTSKUYVA NAMPEYO**
Hopi-Tewa, b. 1928
Jar, 1970-1985
6.5 x 11.25. Purchased by the Heard Museum from Richard Howard, who bought the jar from the artist. NA-SW-HO-A7-159.

*Joseph Lonewolf's avanyu bowl below is a study in ornamental design. The full headdress of the contemporary avanyu flows and moves with the quickness of a lightning storm.*

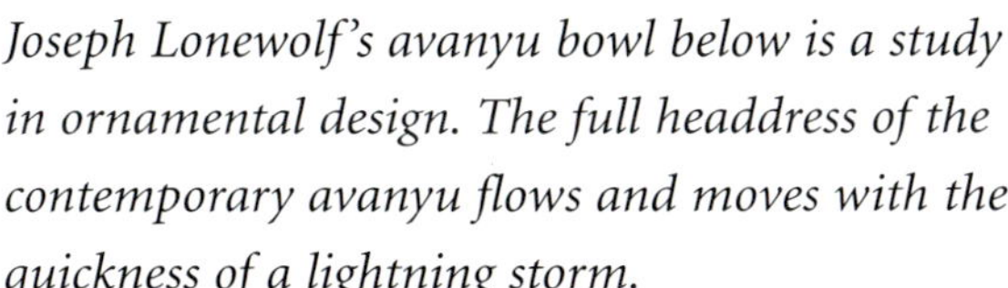

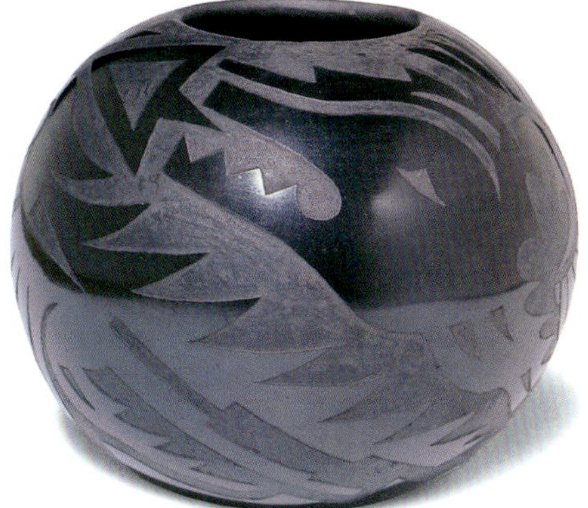

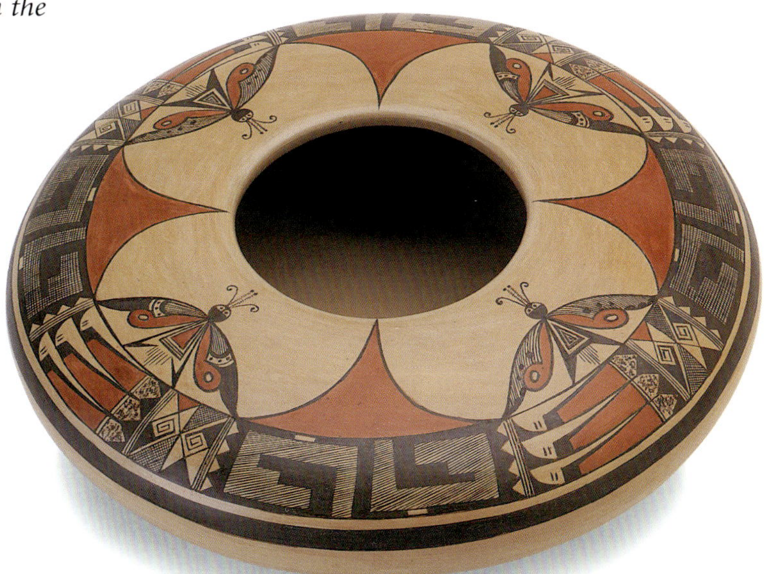

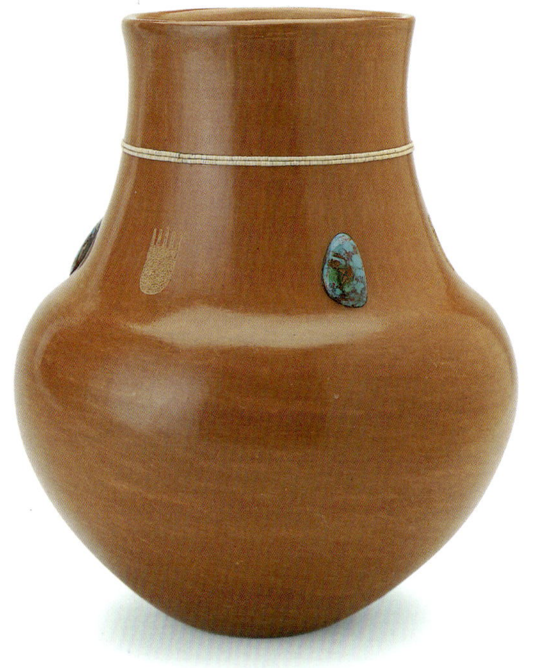

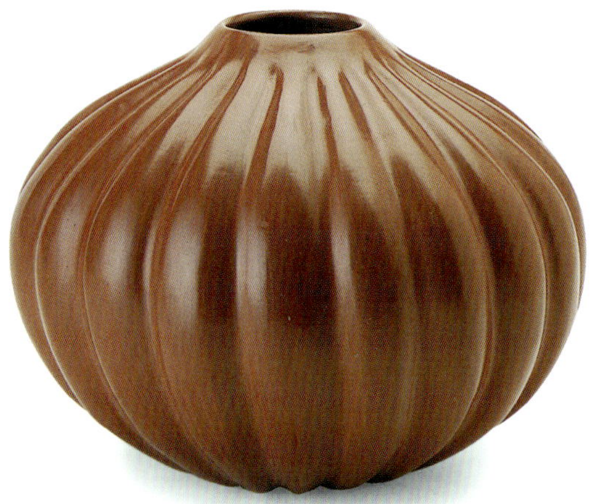

Melons are the fruits of life. This piece was selected not only because of the aesthetic beauty but also because Helen Shupla and Mela Youngblood were the first to introduce the melon-shape pot.

Tony Da's jar is strong, solid and masculine, with a touch of personal ornamentation. This jar particularly depicts the personality of the potter.

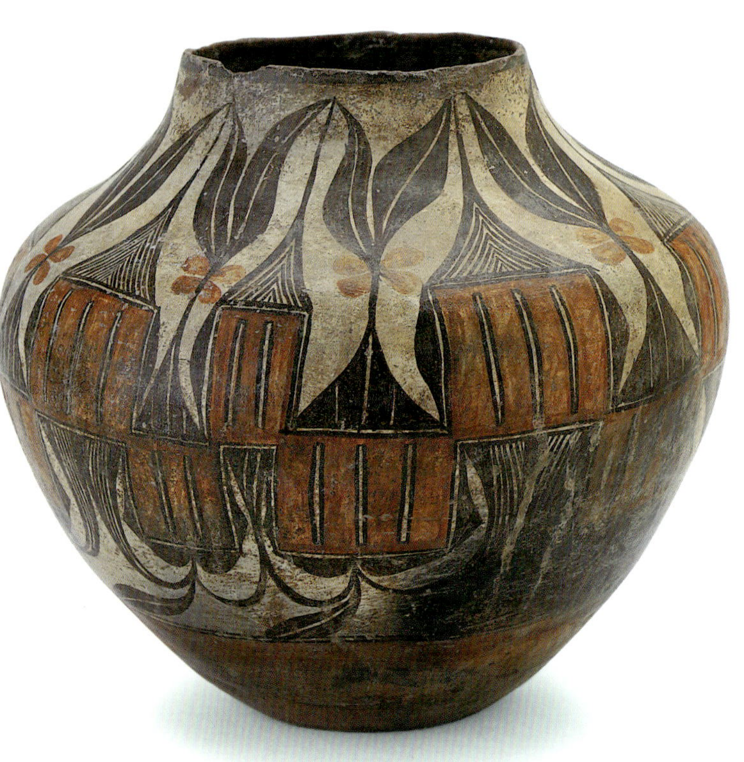

This Zia jar is historically very interesting since the motif appears very Moorish and Euro-Spanish. With the introduction of other cultures into the pueblos, potters have integrated non-pueblo art into their designs.

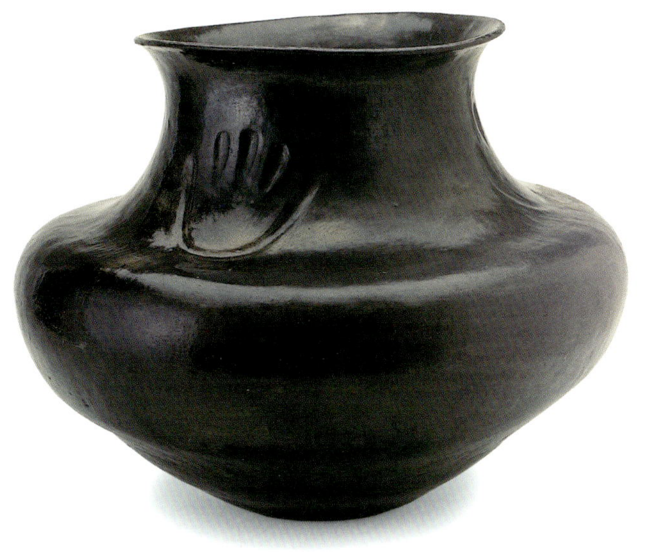

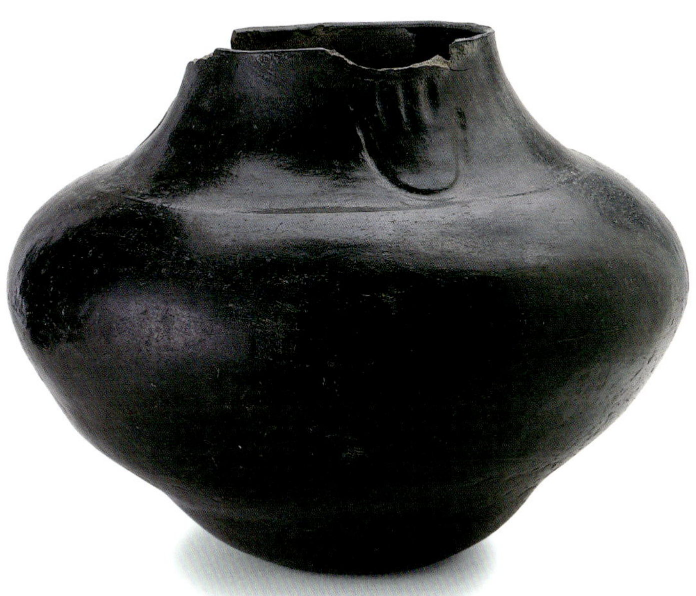

*The size of this jar and the polishing of it make it a masterwork. It is difficult to stone polish a pot this size, or even half this size. It probably took twelve hours just to polish this jar.*

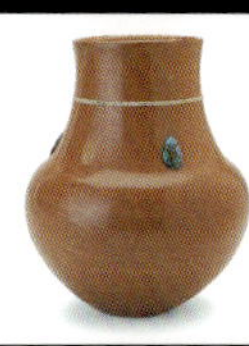

**TONY DA**
**San Ildefonso, b. 1940**
**Jar, 1970s**
14 x 10.3. Acquired by the donors at the Heard Museum Shop. Gift from the Estate of Herman and Claire Blum, 3576-146.

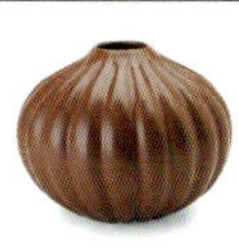

**HELEN SHUPLA**
**Santa Clara, 1928-1985**
**Jar**
9.25 x 12.25. Purchased by the Heard Museum from Richard Howard, who acquired the jar from the artist, NA-SW-SC-A1-14.

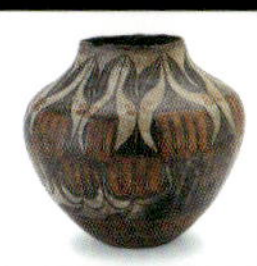

**ZIA JAR, 1870-1875**
12 x 12.75. Date attributed by Dr. Alfred Dittert of Arizona State University, Tempe. Fred Harvey Fine Arts Collection, 235P.

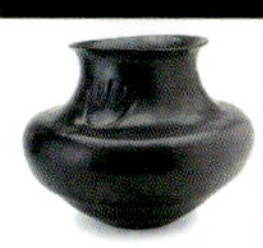

**SANTA CLARA JAR, c. 1915**
16 x 18. Fred Harvey Fine Arts Collection, 560P.

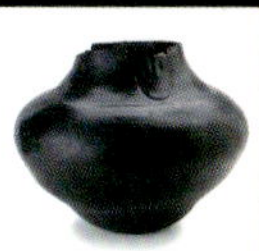

**SANTA CLARA JAR, EARLY 1900s**
19 x 24. Fred Harvey Fine Arts Collection, 181P.

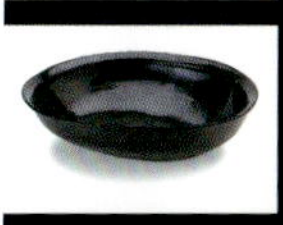

**SANTA CLARA BOWL, EARLY 1900s**
3.75 x 15.5 x 13. Fred Harvey Fine Arts Collection, 581P.

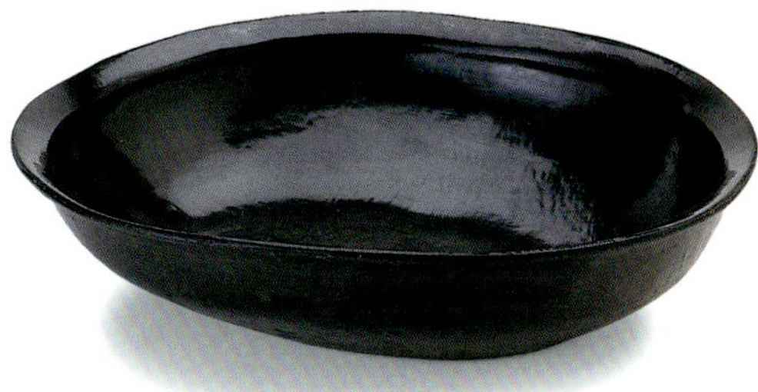

*This oval bowl is incredible due to the angle and thinness of the walls and the high sheen achieved.*

*This early 1900 jar was difficult to shape and form due to the contours. The jar was smoked on the inside and left red on the outside, with the lower base unpolished.*

*Wedding vases like the two below are some of the more interesting and difficult shapes to create. Teresita Naranjo has made the shape of this piece look effortless. Her choice of design in its intricacy lends well to the overall aesthetics of the pot. This piece is a fine example of where "contemporary" deep-carved pieces originated.*

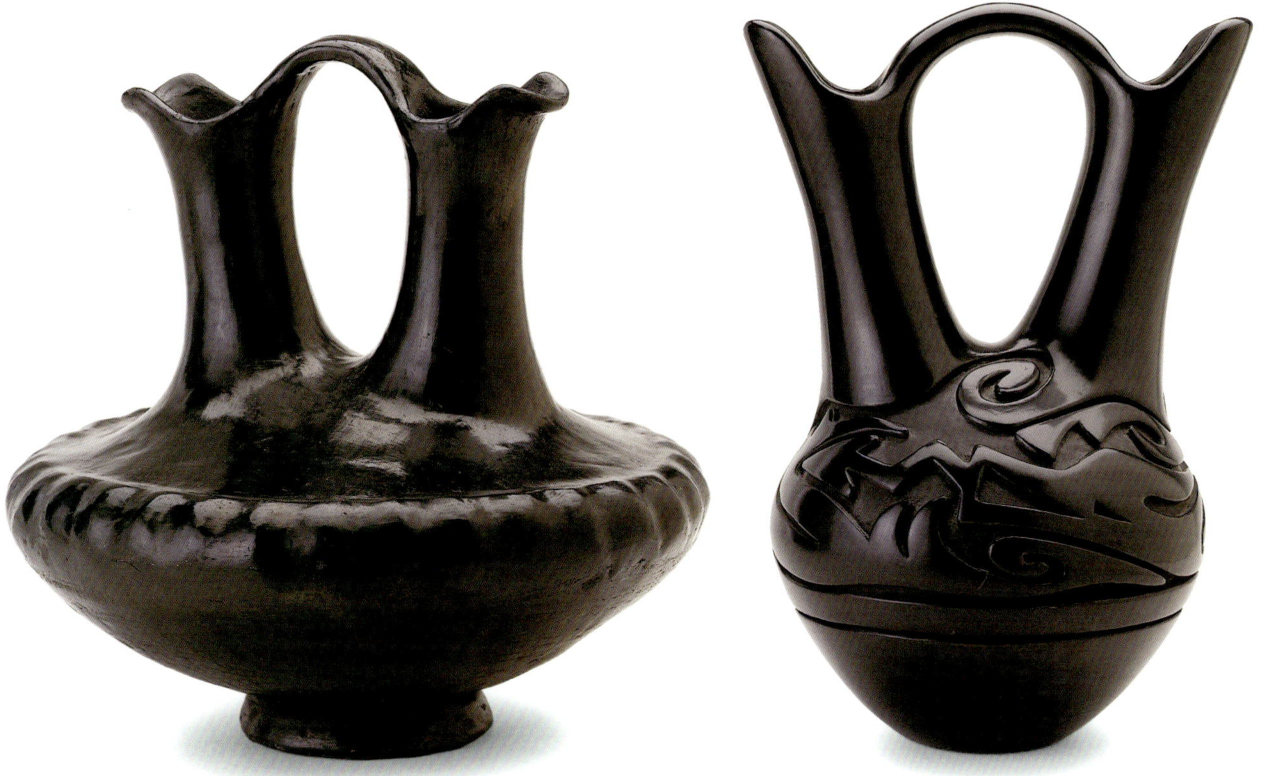

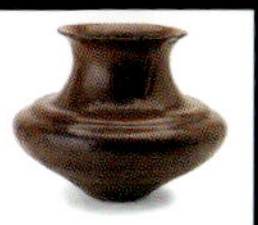

**SANTA CLARA JAR, 1905**

11 x 13. Fred Harvey Fine Arts Collection, 513P.

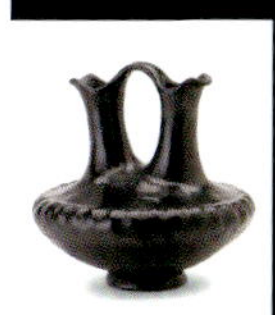

**SANTA CLARA DOUBLE SPOUT VASE, EARLY 1900s**

11 x 11.5. Purchased by Maie Heard prior to 1944. Heard Museum Collection, NA-SW-SC-A10-6.

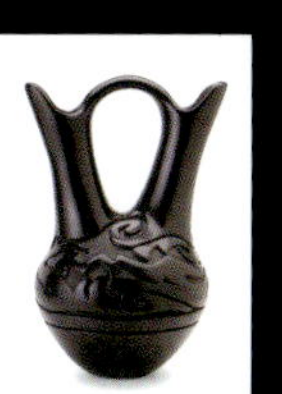

**TERESITA NARANJO**
**Santa Clara, 1919-1999**
**Wedding Vase, 1970s**

15 x 10.5 x 9. Acquired by the donors at the Heard Museum Shop. Gift from the Estate of Herman and Claire Blum, 3576-241.

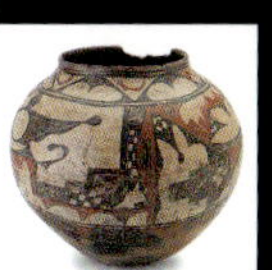

**SANTA ANA JAR, c. 1820-1870**

15 x 16. Acquired by the Harvey Company in the early 1900s from Frederick Volz, a trader at Canyon Diablo, Arizona. Fred Harvey Fine Arts Collection, 116P.

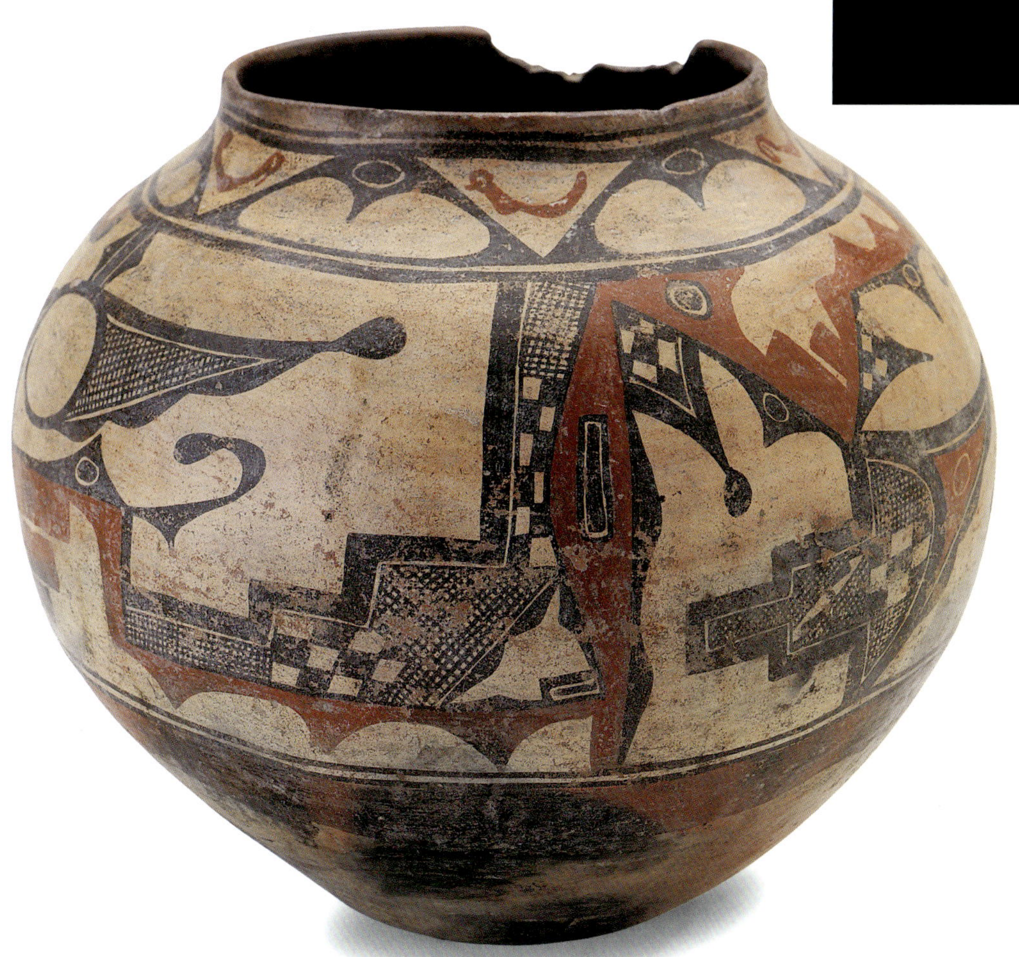

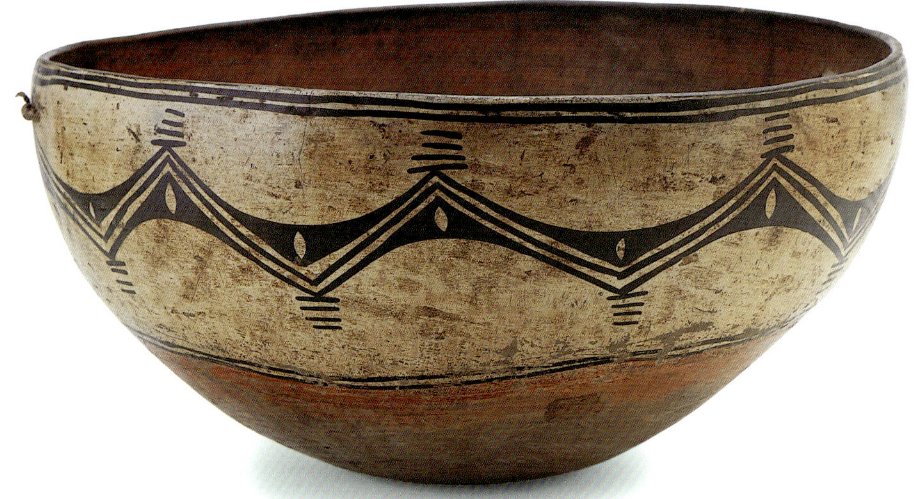

*A thunderstorm is on the horizon, moving to the beat of a drum—vibrating, flowing and calling for the avanyu (water serpent). I have never seen such interesting use of movement in either traditional or contemporary work. The elegant, bold flat lines at the crest of each wave are an ingenious way to suggest movement without great effort.*

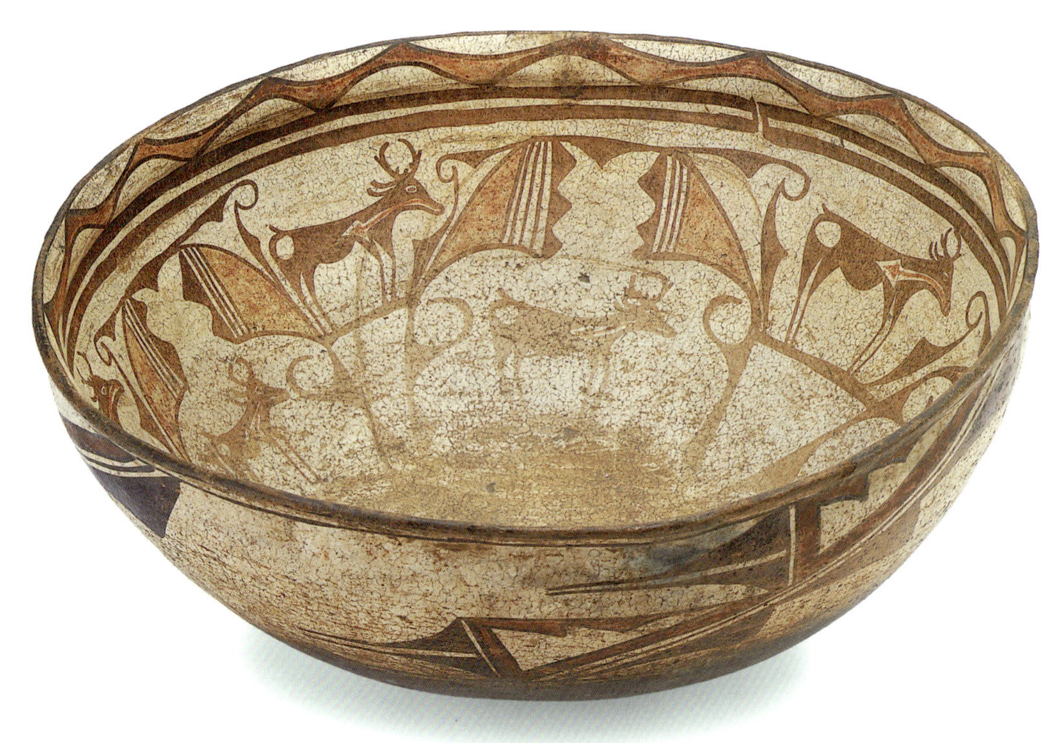

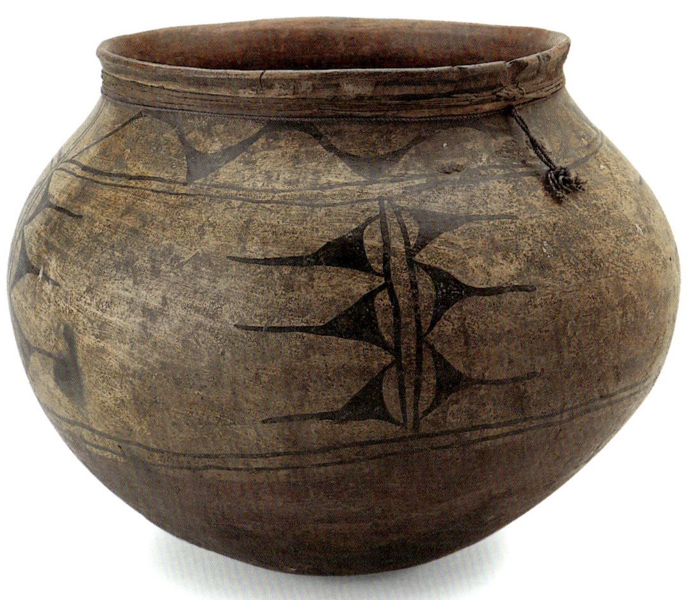

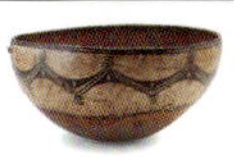

**COCHITI BOWL, c. 1880**

11.5 x 22. Fred Harvey Fine Arts Collection, 135P.

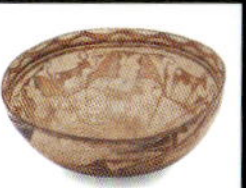

**ZUNI BOWL, LATE 1800s**

9.75 x 20. Acquired by the Harvey Company in the early 1900s from Frederick Volz, a trader at Canyon Diablo, Arizona. Fred Harvey Fine Arts Collection, 115P.

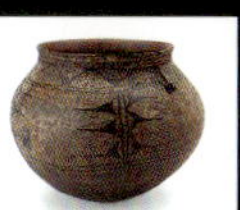

**COCHITI JAR, LATE 1800s**

16 x 20. Fred Harvey Fine Arts Collection, 535P.

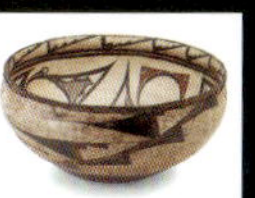

**ZUNI BOWL, 1885-1890**

7 x 17.25. Date attributed by Dr. Alfred Dittert of Arizona State University, Tempe. Fred Harvey Fine Arts Collection, 406P.

*This jar has withstood the test of time in terms of shape and design. The potter displays great self-confidence in her or his technical skill and creative design due to the size of the pot. It is inviting, free and open.*

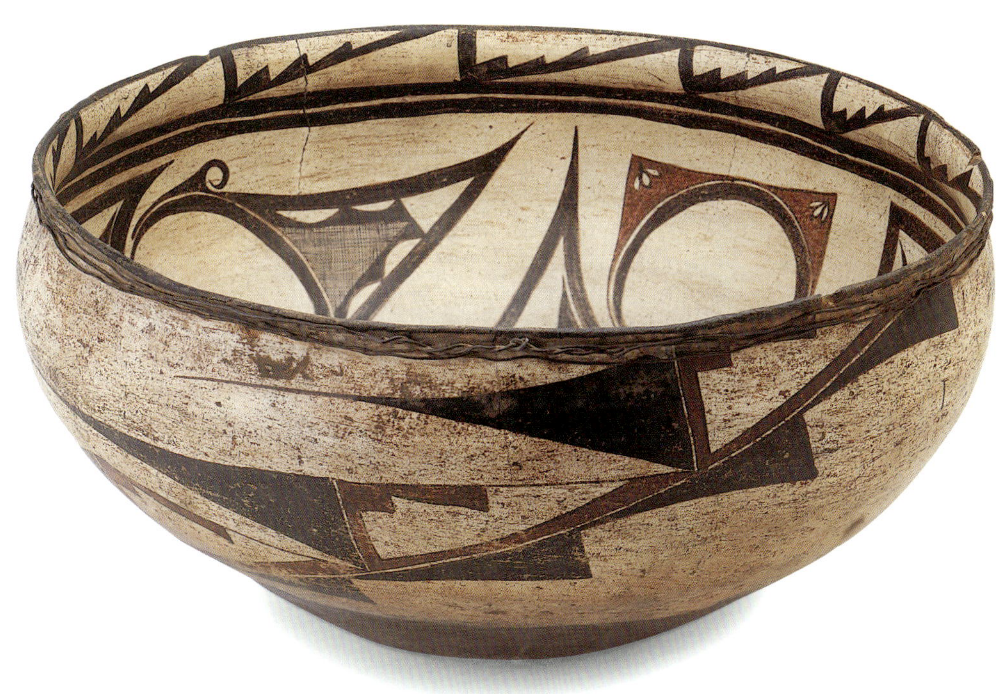

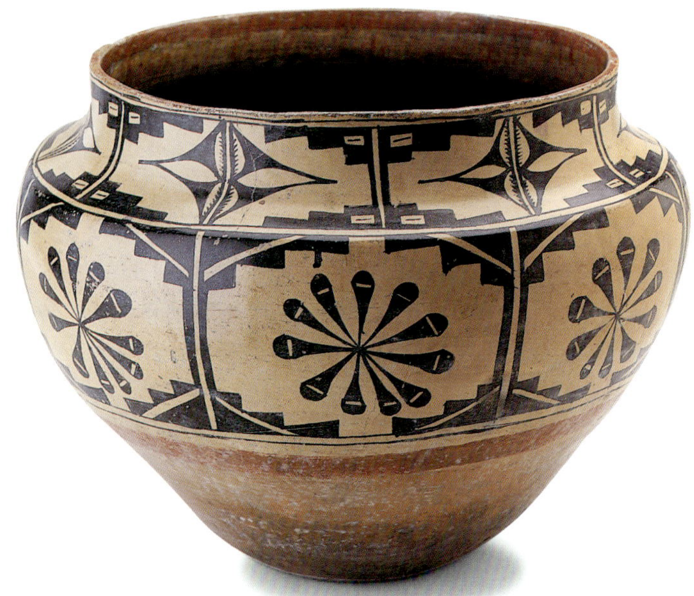

*This Santo Domingo jar is perfection in art; the shape and design is very symmetrical. The design is segmented to accommodate the circular designs in the center, giving a highly pleasing effect.*

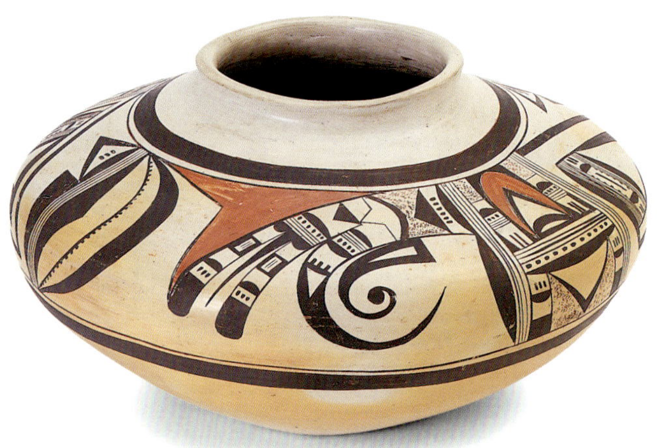

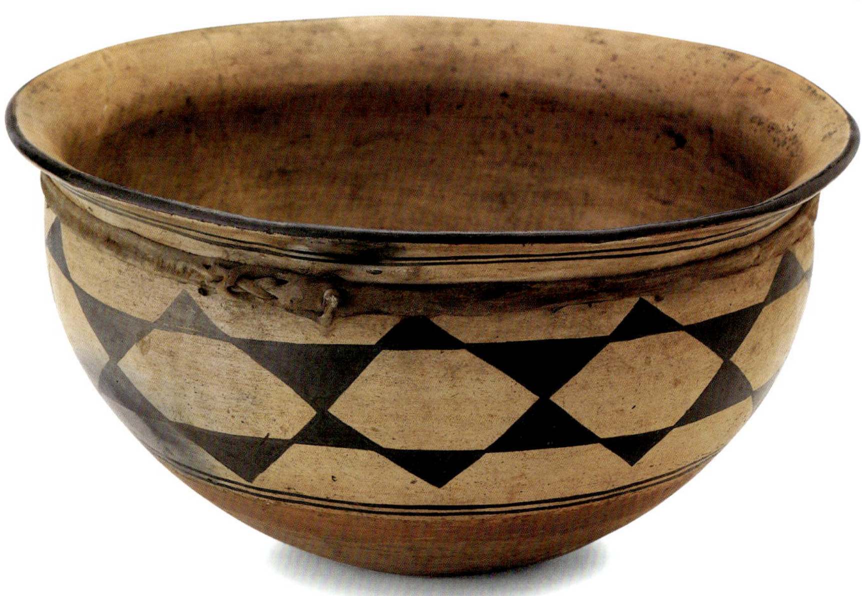

*This large Santo Domingo dough bowl illustrates an excellent example of the process of early pueblo design into illusionary imagery. The motifs look like a star, but on closer observation, they are slanted squares with triangles.*

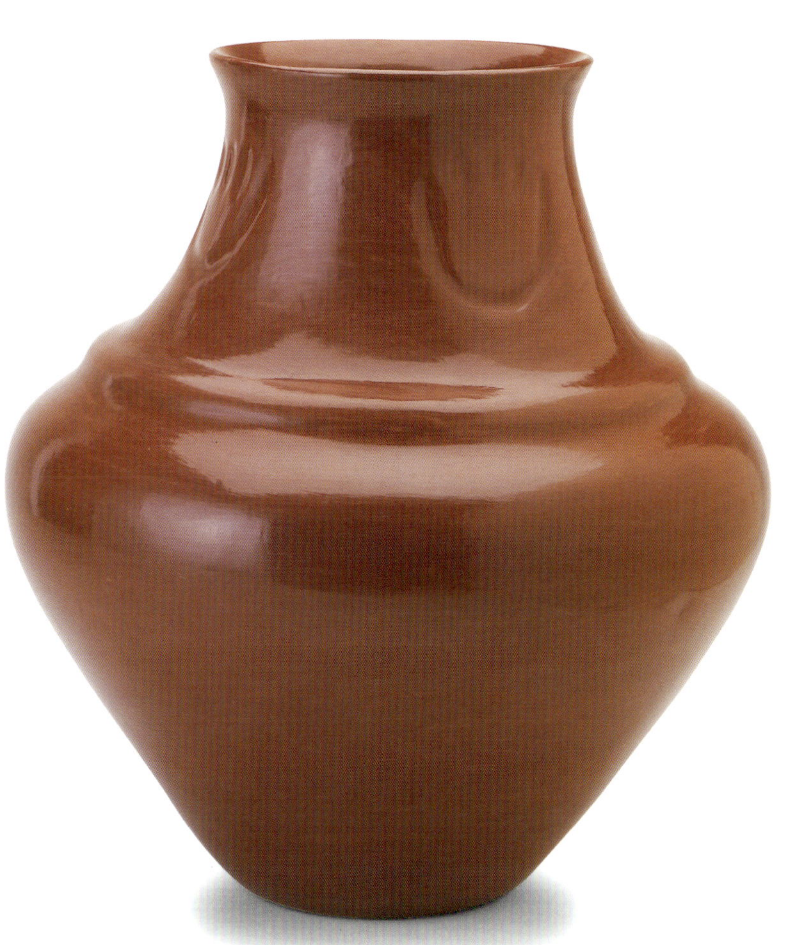

*Margaret Tafoya was amazing at polishing—even in her advanced years.*

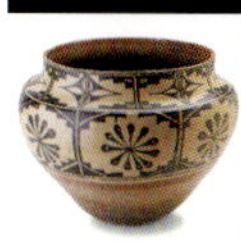

### SANTO DOMINGO JAR, c. 1900

17.5 x 23. This jar appears in photographs taken between 1902 and 1907 at the Harvey Company showroom in the Alvarado Hotel in Albuquerque, New Mexico. It was acquired from Frederick Volz, a trader at Canyon Diablo, Arizona. Fred Harvey Fine Arts Collection, 124P.

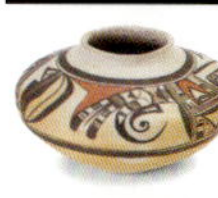

### NAMPEYO
**Hopi-Tewa, 1862-1942**
**Jar, 1920s**

7.875 x 14. Acquired by Maie and Dwight Heard from Herbert and Allie Walling BraMé of the Arizona Curio Company on June 12, 1928.  Although this jar was purchased as the work of Nampeyo, family members have suggested that it may have been made by either Nampeyo's daughter Annie Healing (Hopi-Tewa, 1884-1968) or Healing's daughter Daisy Hooee (Hopi-Tewa, 1906-1994). Heard Museum Collection, NA-SW-HO-A7-30.

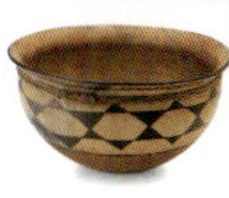

### MONICA SILVA
**Santo Domingo**
**Bowl, early 1900s**

6 x 13.5. Fred Harvey Fine Arts Collection, 455P

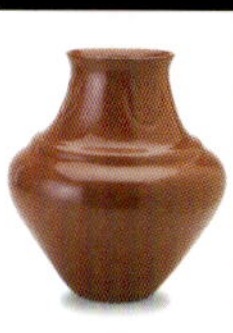

### MARGARET TAFOYA
**Santa Clara, 1904-2001**
**Jar, c. 1973**

14.5 x 12. Purchased by the Heard Museum from the House of Six Directions, Scottsdale, Arizona, NA-SW-SC-A1-8.

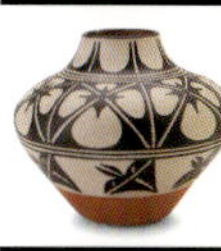

### ROBERT TENORIO
**Santo Domingo**
**Jar, 2001**

10 x 11. Gift of the artist, 4098-1.

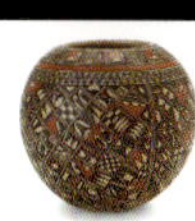

### RONDINA HUMA
**Hopi-Tewa, b. 1947**
**Jar, 1994**

6.875 x 7.25. Acquired by the donors at the Heard Museum Shop. Gift of Richard and Carolyn Morgan, 4043-34.

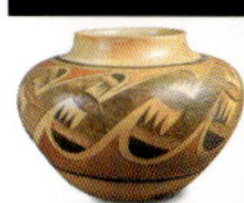

### FANNIE NAMPEYO
**Hopi-Tewa, 1900-2000**
**Jar, 1930s**

20 x 26. Acquired by the donors with the purchase of Tom Pavatea's shop at Polacca, Arizona, in 1948. Gift of William and Louise McGee, 4054-1.

*Robert Tenorio's pot has a breath of tradition but forges into another realm of change by reworking traditional designs and enhancing the negative space.*

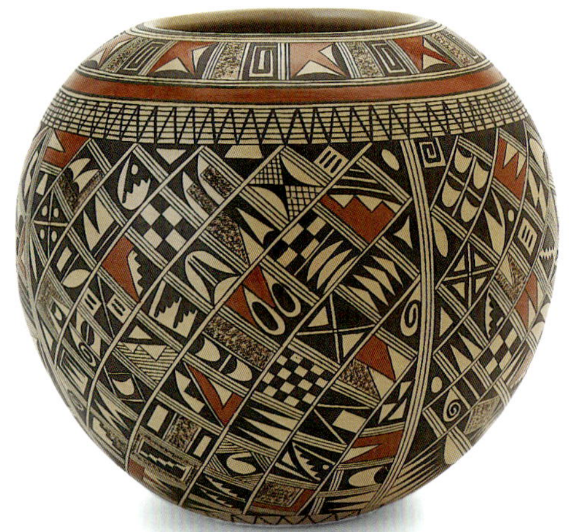

*This is a pot of great beauty and intricate design. Rondina Huma consistently reveals her technical skill and patience while working with the clay.*

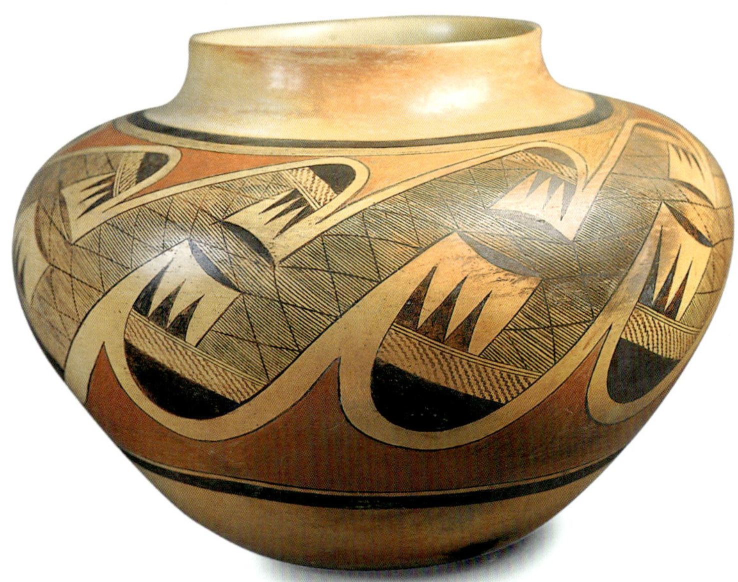

*This jar is breathtaking. Imagine living in a pot this size. Imagine coiling, polishing and painting on this pot! Its width at the shoulder is twenty-six inches and it stands twenty inches tall.*

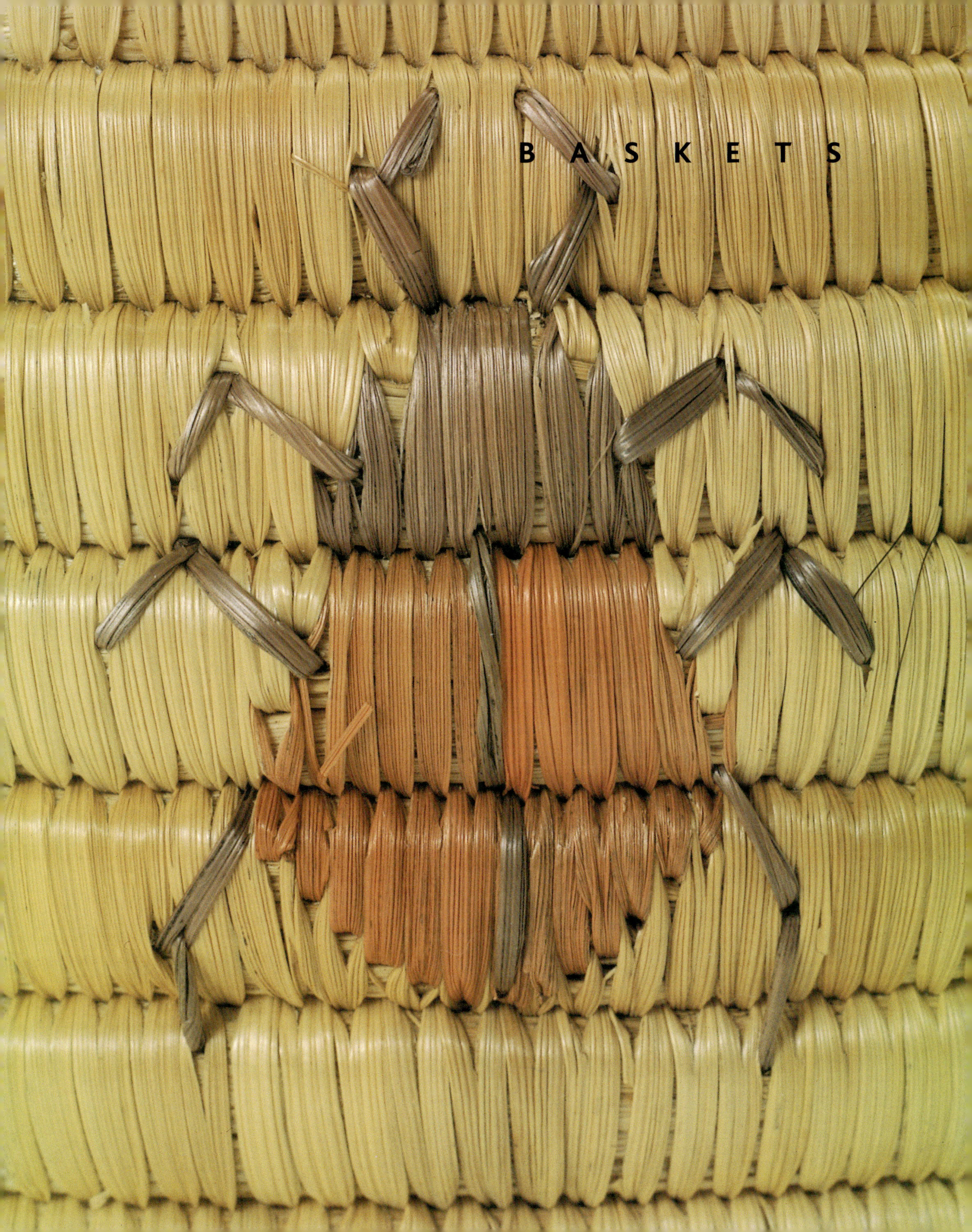

B A S K E T S

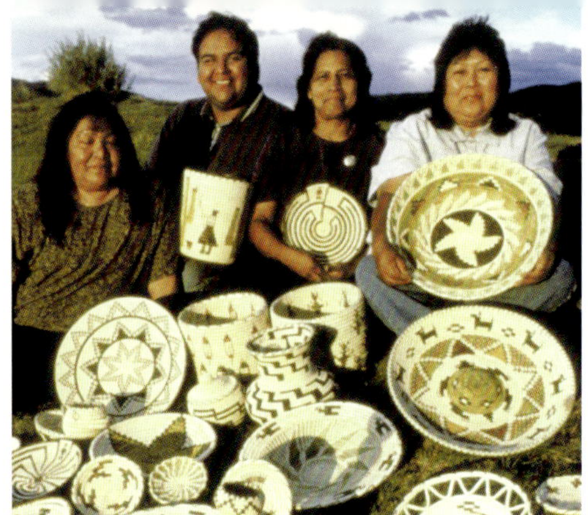



# BASKETRY

## WEAVING THE DREAM

### BY TERROL DEW JOHNSON AND TRISTAN READER

I WAS A DREAM WEAVER before I ever picked up my first awl or placed my first stitch. As a child, I sat on the floor of my family's home, looking at all the photos of baskets that covered the pages of my father's Reader's Digest book series about Native Americans. It was then that I began to dream baskets. Patterns, textures and styles began to fill my head as I slept, calling out to me in the language of fibers. To this day, these dreams of the vast artistic and cultural diversity of basketry traditions drive me. My elders and teachers such as Clara Javier, Loretta Manuel and Margaret Acosta have brought dreams of a rich past to life. Their generosity has helped me learn more than just the techniques of weaving. It

has helped me understand the heritage of hard work, culture and artistic vision that has driven generations of my ancestors to live artfully in the dry desert.

Today, my own baskets—both contemporary and traditional—often emerge from the dream process. New designs and styles haunt my sleep, calling me to weave them into the waking world, one stitch at a time, until they have taken on a life of their own. And even with the many challenges to the survival of our Native traditions, the dream of a vibrant future for basketry is being woven by the many young weavers who I have had the honor to teach—weavers who combine respect for the lessons of a rich heritage with their own dreams and visions. For me, the fibers of a basket weave together the dream world and the material world, connecting the past, present and future.

In the Tohono O'odham language, we have no word for art. My ancestors never really created formal artwork that was separated from day-to-day life. Instead, Native people have always looked to create artful ways of living, seeking ways to blend beauty and use-fulness. We try to live in ways that bring together the material, spiritual and aesthetic worlds. In basketry, beauty and utility are joined together. Some call it art; most bas-ketweavers simply call it life. This heritage presented me with a challenge in choosing baskets that were "masterworks." How can that one word include everything from a gigantic Pima grain storage basket to my people's ceremonial wine baskets and today's "art baskets"? Baskets have been created for so many purposes: utility, trade, ceremony and artistry. As I searched through the hundreds of baskets in the Heard Museum collection, I kept asking myself, "What makes a basket a masterwork when there is such a variety of purposes, styles and cultural traditions within Native basketry traditions?" Finally, two answers came to me.

First, a masterwork is simply a basket that fully expresses the weaver's vision. A basket created only for artistic reasons may be judged upon aesthetic considerations alone. But a basket designed for work—to winnow grain or to catch a fish, for example—has to be judged on the weaver's ability to fashion the natural fibers provided by the land into a useful tool. When these tools also are beautiful and express the weaver's artistic vision, then I call them masterworks.

Second, and for me more important, is the way in which a basket's story tells us about the life of the weaver and the life of our Native communities. My elders have always told stories in order to teach us lessons. Each of the baskets in this collection represents the inspiration and vision of a weaver.

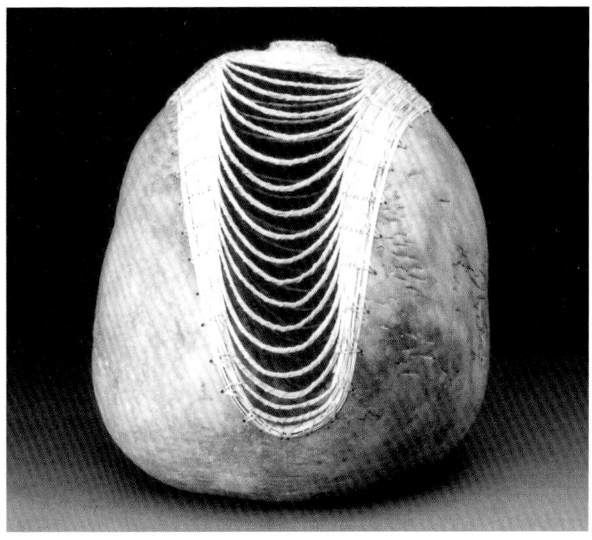

Terrol Dew Johnson, Tohono O'odham, b. 1971. Gourd basket with beargrass, 2000. 15 x 12.

We know some of their names and stories. But more of them are anonymous, their identities and life stories lost to us forever. Yet, when I think of the hope, love, labor, spirit, tears and laughter that have gone into each of these baskets, I begin to think in new ways about what makes something a masterwork. In the fibers of these baskets, we glimpse the worlds of the weavers, their daily lives, their labor, their culture, their visions as artful people. It is those stories that helped me select these masterpieces. And it is through those stories that I can share my vision of this exhibit.

## Seeing the Masterwork

Looking back on the process of selecting the baskets for this exhibit, I once again wondered what makes a masterwork. Finally, the teaching of one of my elders provided me with the answer. One day many years ago, I saw my teacher Clara Javier near her home. By then she had completely lost her eyesight. Sadly, she could no longer weave. But she asked to hold the basket I had just completed. Her hands ran over the surface, feeling the smoothness of the coil. Then she held it to her nose and inhaled the smells of the desert. Smiling, she handed it back to me. "It is beautiful," she said simply.

Maybe that is what makes a basket a masterwork. When you look with your eyes or your hands or your heart and you see its beauty.

## The Four Winds of Basketry

Within my Tohono O'odham culture, the four directions play an important role in our ceremonial life. We dance facing each of the four directions, repeating each of our sacred songs four times. For me, each direction brings different winds and influences. In the same way, the arrangement of this exhibit represents the four winds and influences of our basketry traditions: utility, trade, ceremony and artistry. These four winds represent the world of Native basketry.

Tristan Reader is a co-founder of TOCA and works closely with Tohono O'odham community members to revitalize cultural traditions. As co-directors of TOCA, Terrol Dew Johnson and Tristan Reader collaborate on many projects.

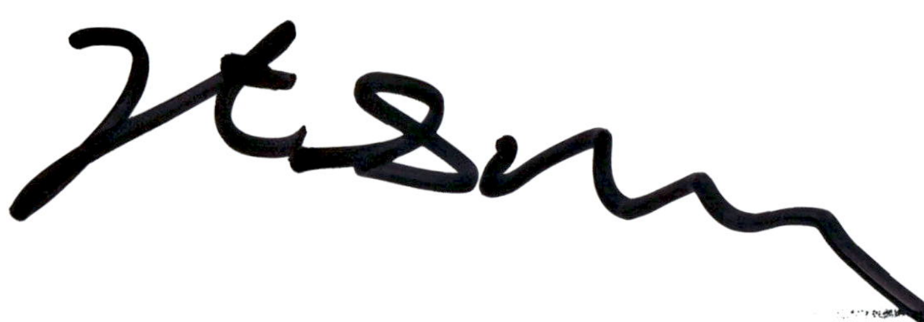

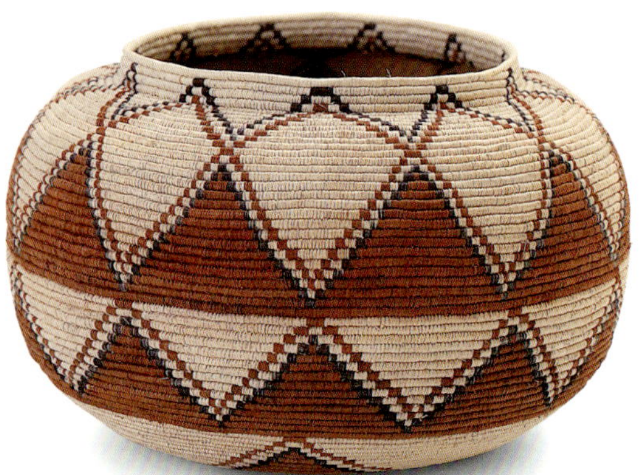

**MARIA ESTER MOLINA**
**Seri, Punta Chueca, Sonora**
**Polychrome basket, c. 1978**

5.75 x 8.5; 9 coils/inch, 26 stitches/inch. Close coiled on torote bundle foundation with dyed and undyed torote fiber sewing element. Heard Museum Purchase, NA-SW-SE-B-13.

*South of the border, the Seri are still making some of the finest coiled baskets. They still use bone awls and sing songs over each finished basket. When a huge basket—more than three feet tall—is completed, the whole village holds a celebration. They have a vibrant and living tradition.*

# Utility

T HE FOUNDATION of all basketry traditions is utility. For countless generations, the woven basket has been an important tool for everything from cooking to building our cultures. At home, baskets have been used to carry water, prepare food and store household items. Beyond these types of household uses, their light weight and durability have ensured their critical role in the development of the different lifeways of Native peoples. My own people's use of burden baskets made our annual migration from our mountain villages to our farming villages possible; I cannot imagine such a long trip with people carrying their possessions in heavy, fragile pottery. The usefulness of baskets is so important that the burden basket made its way into the legends told to me by my elders.

LEGEND OF THE BASKET

One day, I'itoi—Elder Brother—sent a messenger deep under the ground, looking for a people who would help him defeat his enemies. In response, the O'odham—the People—journeyed to the earth's surface. But they were not alone as they emerged through an opening in the ground; each person was followed by a burden basket walking on its own four legs. Heavily loaded with all of the people's possessions, the baskets scampered here and there, bearing the weight so that the People could move to assist I'itoi more quickly.

**AKIMEL O'ODHAM BURDEN BASKET, 1900-1925**

26 x 22. Saguaro rib, willow, maguey fiber, agave leaf, yucca, horsehair cord. Gift of Mrs. Gregg Scott, NA-SW-PI-B-316.

*This burden basket must have carried everything from firewood to a sleeping child. It was made for hard use, but the colors incorporated into the weaving are beautiful. Unfortunately, only one or two weavers today still know how to make these carriers of culture.*

From high atop a nearby mountain, the trickster Ban—Coyote—watched all of this in amazement. He was startled to see the People and their baskets emerge from the earth. But Coyote had the power to change things simply by laughing at them. So, as the O'odham passed by the foot of the mountain, Coyote laughed at them. "Ha, ha, ha," he chuckled. "The baskets are doing all of the work."

As soon as Coyote spoke these words, the baskets dropped their heavy loads and stopped walking. Although the O'odham helped defeat I'itoi's enemies that day, baskets never walked again. Ever since, Tohono O'odham women have carried their heavy loads themselves. But still today, the baskets remain where they stopped, a place called Quijotoa—Burden Basket Mountain.

Whenever I look out across the desert at the peaks of Quijotoa, I am reminded of the importance of baskets as a tool of survival in the Sonoran Desert. My people used them to winnow grain, to parch corn, to store crops, to carry firewood, to embrace our babies. Despite the useful nature of baskets, the artful way of living is contained in each stitch. I am constantly inspired by the ways in which weavers of all tribes bring their artistic vision to weaving such simple and basic tools.

There have been so many practical uses of baskets. But some represent much more than just daily life. One basket in particular represents for me the many hopes and struggles of my own people. When I first saw the giant grain storage basket in the Heard Museum collection, I was deeply moved by the labor of love that it must have been. The weaver saved the straw left over after the harvest of winter wheat and stripped the tough bark off mesquite trees in order to weave such a huge basket. The vision of weavers using the leftover stalks of wheat to make a container for the grain shows how O'odham have always found ways to create useful things from the desert.

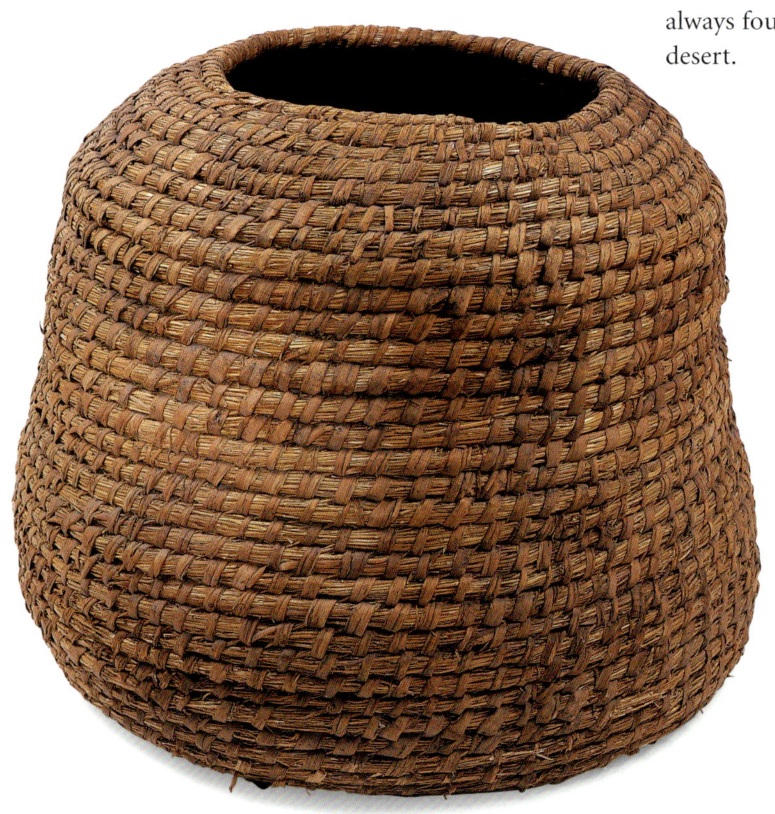

**AKIMEL O'ODHAM GRAIN STORAGE BASKET, c. 1900**

31.5 x 33.5; 1 coil/inch. Open coiled of wheat straw with mesquite bark sewing element. Fred Harvey Fine Arts Collection, 816BA.

*This basket is one of my favorites. When government agents came to take our children to boarding schools, parents would hide the children in these huge baskets. The rest of the time, they held grain. These baskets preserved the O'odham family both by preserving the fruits of the harvest and by protecting our families from the pain of separation and forced assimilation.*

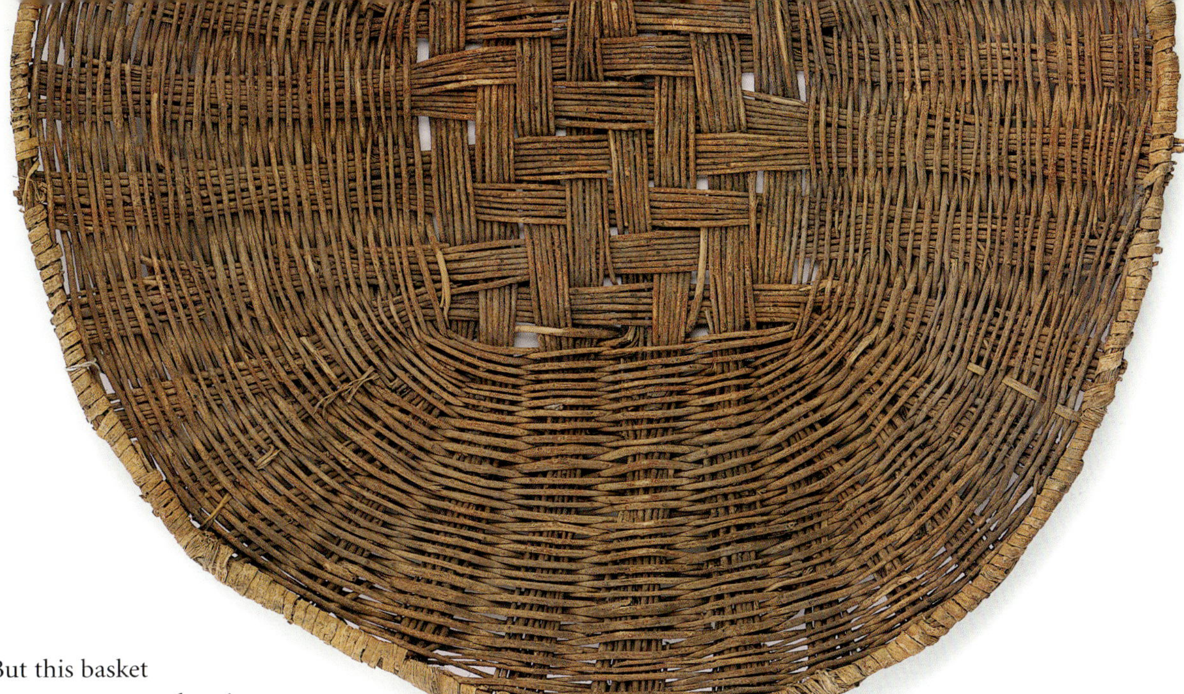

**HOPI TRAY, c. 1900**

1.5 x 15.75. Sumac with a plaited center and wicker sides, yucca wrapped rim. Purchased by the Fred Harvey Company from Charles Owen, assistant curator, Field Museum. Collected at Shipaulovi, Second Mesa, Arizona, 449CI-17.

But this basket represents more than just a tool for storing grain; it is also a tool of cultural survival. For decades, government agents would come to all O'odham villages to take the children away to boarding schools, where they were punished for speaking our language and practicing our culture. Looking at the basket in the basement of the museum, I remember the stories of parents who would hide their children from the government agents in storage baskets just like this. These were parents who loved their children and did not want to lose them, parents who did not want their children to lose their language and culture. Even though this basket may not be the most "beautiful" basket in the eyes of the art world, it served my people well, preserving our food and our people for generations. It is truly a masterwork.

*These baskets were created as tools for the chores of everyday life, yet they are so artful, showing the ways in which weavers incorporate beauty into all aspects of their lives.*

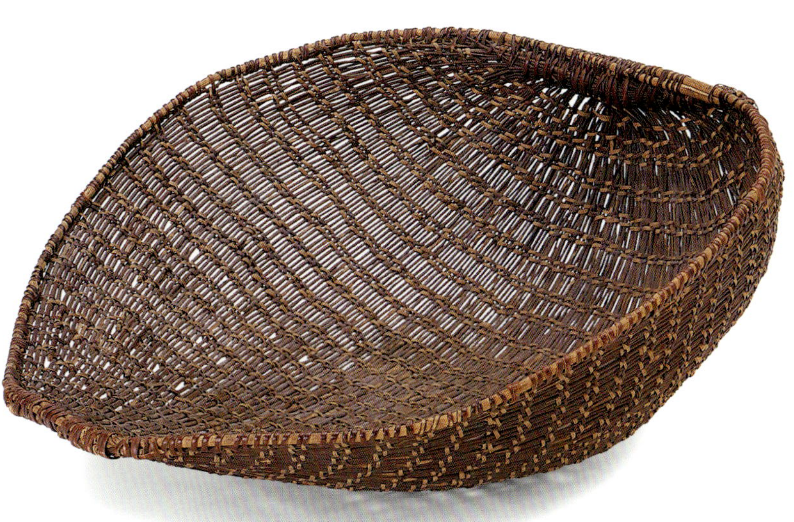

**SOUTHERN YOKUTS SCOOP, c. 1950**

18.5 x 17.5. Open twined of sheathed and unsheathed redbud. Gift of Mr. and Mrs. Byron Harvey III, NA-CB-TU-B-5.

*The simple and elegant shape of this basket follows its function. The subtle patterning created by using redbud is wonderful. When well made, even the most basic utilitarian baskets are beautiful.*

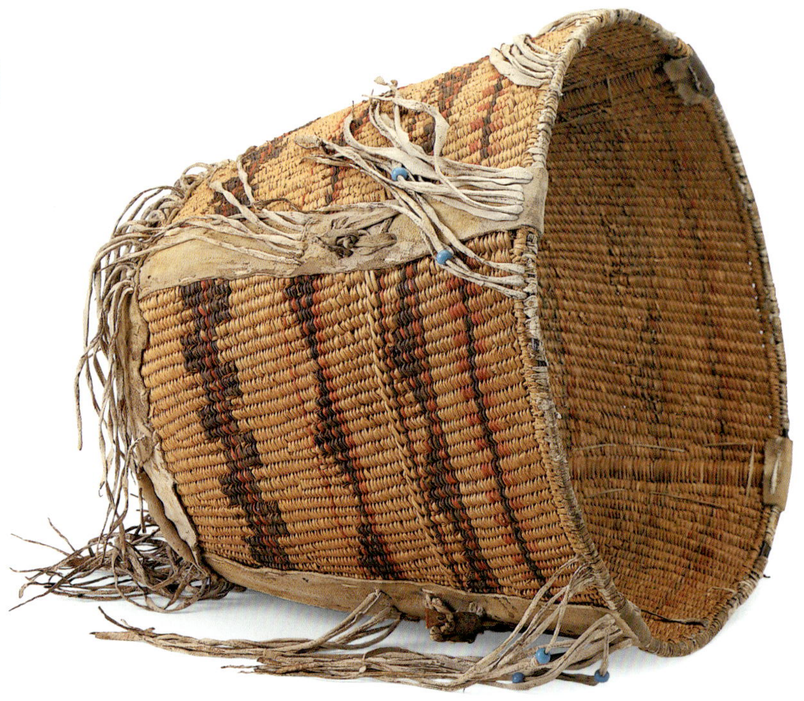

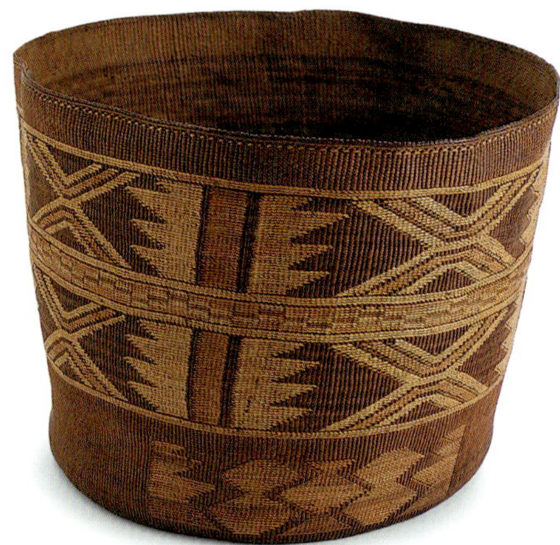

*The naturally tanned leather of this basket is a clue to its history. It was made with great care, incorporating both the natural resources of the weaver's world and beads obtained through trade.*

*This basket shows how much effort weavers put into making very practical tools beautiful. It is still alive, holding the spirit of the weaver. With these old baskets, we have to hold them, touch them, talk to them. We have to let them know we are here.*

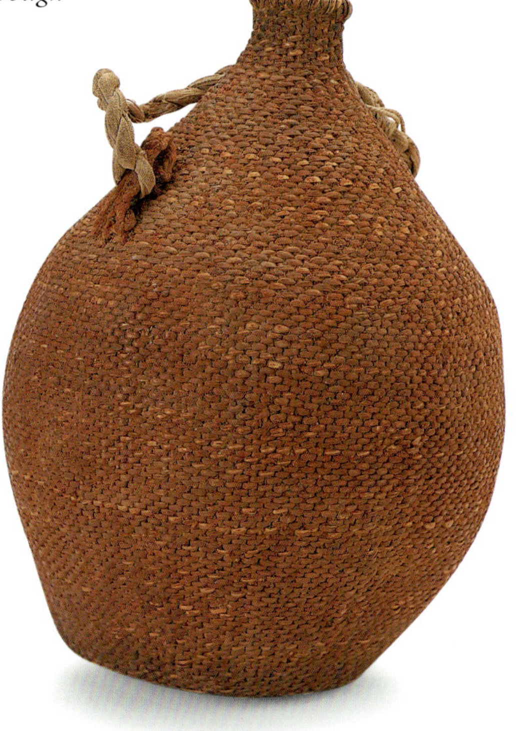

*This pitched water bottle has a great flowing form. Even though the pitch has worn off, we are left with a wonderful color. This simple and useful basket has stood the test of time. After years and years of use, it is still here a hundred years after the weaver created it. That alone makes it a masterwork.*

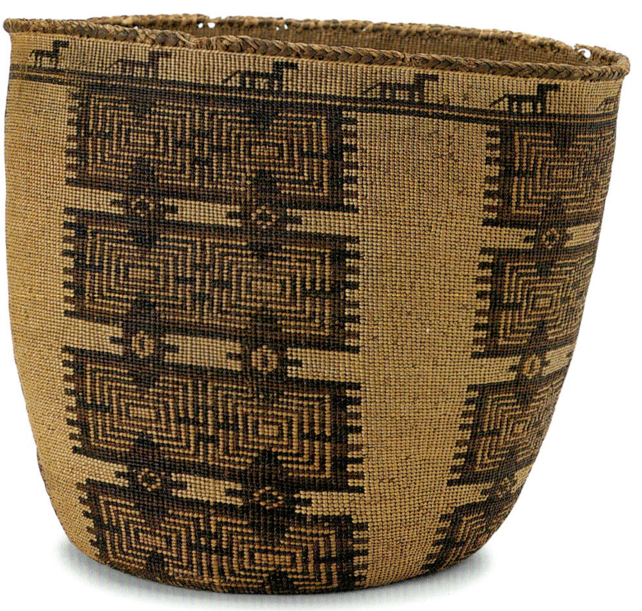

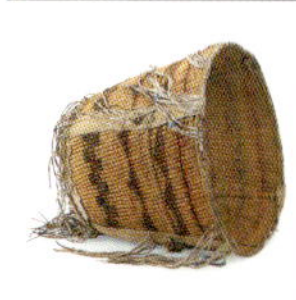

**WESTERN APACHE BURDEN BASKET, c. 1900**

16.25 x 14.5; 3 warps/inch, 10 wefts/inch. Closed twined of willow with buckskin, glass beads, aniline dyes. Purchased by the Heard Museum prior to 1952 at the Osborn Trading Post in Bylas, Arizona. NA-SW-AP-B-12.

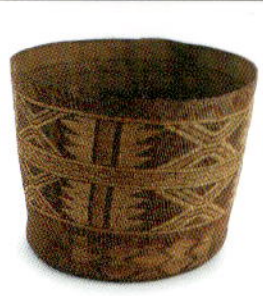

**TLINGIT BASKET, c. 1850**

11 x 15; 9 warps/inch, 13 wefts/inch. Closed twined spruce root basket with a beargrass false embroidery design with fabric handles on the interior. Acquired by the Fred Harvey Company from the Comstock collection, 14BA.

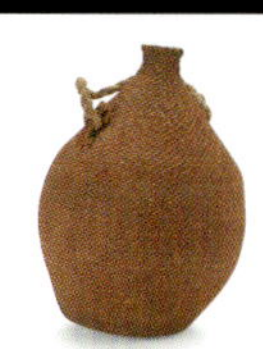

**HUALAPAI WATER BOTTLE, c. 1900**

9.5 x 7; 9 warps/inch, 12 wefts/inch. Closed twined of squawberry or sumac, red mineral clay, piñon pitch, cloth carrying handle. Heard Museum Collection, NA-SW-WA-B-11.

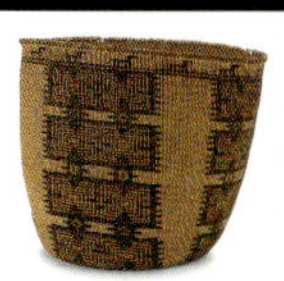

**TWANA PICTORIAL BASKET, c. 1900**

12.5 x 13; 10 warps/inch, 12 wefts/inch. Three-strand twined of cattail and spruce root with beargrass overlay. Heard Museum Collection, NA-NW-SK-B-6.

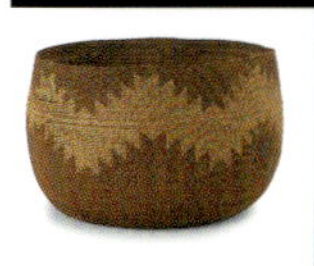

**YUROK COOKING BASKET, 1880-1890**

7.25 x 11; 9 warps/inch, 12 wefts/inch. Half-twist overlay twining of hazel warps and conifer wefts with beargrass design. Gift of Ms. Hally F. Pixley, NA-CB-YU-B-18.

*At one time, this basket had handles and must have been used on a daily basis. It is soft and flexible like cloth, but was made to last; it survived many years of use. And the beauty and complexity of the design shows the weaver's desire to live daily life in an artful way.*

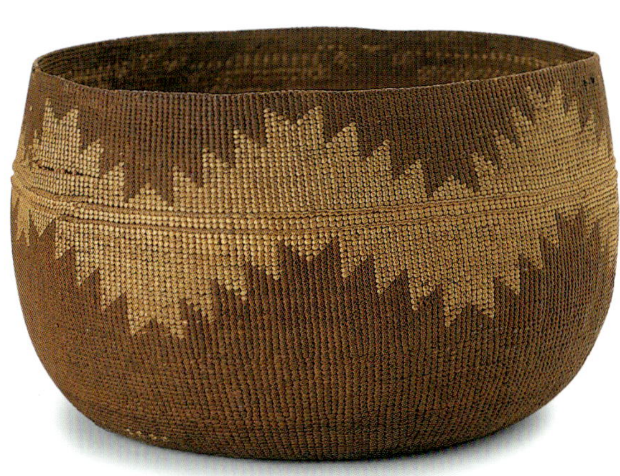

*This basket was clearly used for cooking many meals, but the weaver cared about aesthetics as well as usefulness. It is an example of the artistic vision and self-expression embraced in everyday life.*

NATIVE PEOPLE have always traded with each other, and baskets have always been a valued part of our exchanges. And for more than one hundred years, trade with non-Native peoples has been an important part of the experience of basketweavers. In many ways, trade has made deep and lasting impacts on our weaving traditions.

For centuries, we have given baskets as gifts, used them as prizes for athletic competitions, and even gambled with them. Because each basket contains the good thoughts and energy of the weaver, baskets are as highly valued by our people today as they were by previous generations. The walls of our homes are often covered with baskets given to us by friends and family, baskets that we cherish. I remember how years ago I went without sleep for two days in order to weave a good luck basket that I could give away to my grandmother before she went into the hospital for surgery. I wove my love and good thoughts for her into that basket. To give a basket is not just to give an object; it is to give away a part of who we are.

# Trade

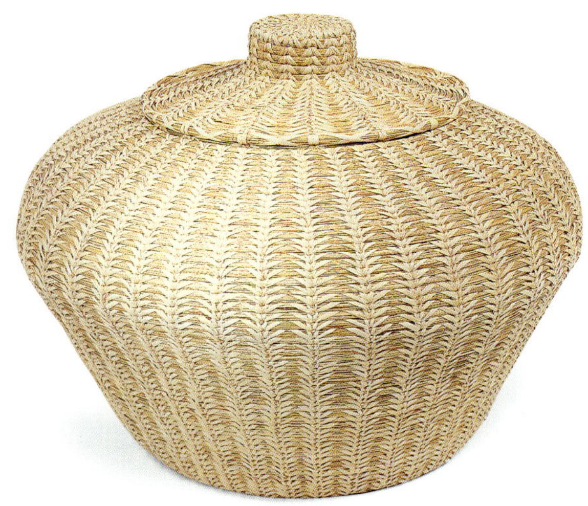

**TOHONO O'ODHAM BASKET WITH LID, 1974**

17.5 x 23; 4 coils/inch. Split-stitch coiled basket with a beargrass bundle and a bleached yucca sewing element. Acquired by the donors at the Santa Rosa Trading Post, Sells, Arizona. Gift of Mr. and Mrs. Glenn E. Quick, Sr., NA-SW-PG-B-99A,B.

*There is more to this basket than first meets the eye. The weaver completed one full coil by weaving in one direction, then returned in the opposite direction to place an additional stitch. This is what created the stitching. This basket is a descendent of the large grain storage basket. It takes the same techniques and refines them.*

As important as trade within our own communities has been, baskets have also been sold to non-Native tourists and collectors for more than a century. The influence of these markets for our work has been both very positive and, at times, highly negative and destructive.

The interests and aesthetics of tourists and collectors has been an important contribution to the innovation and development of basketry traditions. In fact, one of the most significant developments in Tohono O'odham basketry is the result of the tourist market. As more and more tourists traveled to the West in the early part of the 20th century, many wanted to purchase Native American crafts. Unfortunately, many travelers did not value these pieces very much; they just thought of them as souvenirs. But each of our traditional baskets took days and weeks to weave, meaning that weavers would receive just pennies for weeks of work. But then inspiration struck some unknown Tohono O'odham weaver. For generations, the inner coil of grain storage baskets was exposed by spacing stitches far apart, rather than by placing each stitch next to the previous one. Why not just use the same technique for tourist baskets? During the period of great innovation that began in the 1930s, weavers drew inspiration from these giant utilitarian containers and applied the same weaving techniques on a much smaller scale. After all, each of these split-stitch baskets had many fewer stitches than the more traditional baskets and took a fraction of the time to weave. And tourists paid the same price. From these humble origins grew the split-stitch baskets of today, baskets that are wonderful examples of Native artistry. Their complex geometric patterns—particularly stars and sunrays—are simply variations on those of the utilitarian baskets. Today, collectors continue to stimulate creativity within our basketry traditions, and often they are the first to appreciate innovation within basketry, pushing weavers to new heights of creativity and quality.

On the other hand, weavers' experiences of the trading of their baskets have not always been so positive. Non-Native traders often take advantage of the isolation of weavers and their lack of access to markets by paying them unfairly low prices for

their hard work and artistry. A few years ago, one elderly Tohono O'odham weaver from a remote village had created a huge basket with the saguaro harvest design so popular with collectors. For weeks she waited for the trader to come to her village to purchase the basket. Finally, she hitchhiked to a tribally owned trading post. "How much do you want for it?" asked the tribe's buyer. "Well," replied the elder, "I usually get $60 or $70 for ones this big." The buyer was shocked; baskets like that usually sell for $1500 or more. As the elder held $800 in her fist, she quietly said, "all of these years." Then she just cried.

For too many weavers, this situation has been common. But in recent years, many of us have been working to find new ways to market our work collaboratively through cooperatives. Some weavers are even exploring ways of marketing on the Internet. Maybe that is just the next step in the continuing influence of trade on our lives.

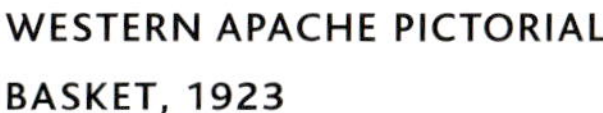

**WESTERN APACHE PICTORIAL BASKET, 1923**

5.25 x 14.25; 5 coils/inch, 20 stitches/inch. Close coiled on a three-rod willow foundation with willow, devil's claw and tree yucca root sewing elements. Fred Harvey Fine Arts Collection, 950BA.

*The rippling motion of the flags gives this basket movement. I would love to know the story behind it. Was it a gift for a visiting government official? Did it commemorate a personal event in the life of someone in the military? Or was it made to appeal to the patriotism of tourists? The materials are so even; the willow has been run through a sizer.*

*The creativity and humor of the weaver are seen in this piece. To create a piece like this—with so many layers and elements— is a challenge. Weavers took traditional techniques that were developed for utilitarian baskets and turned them into pieces such as this.*

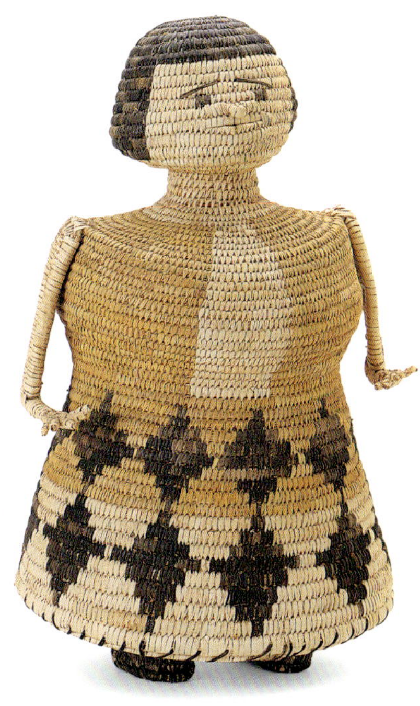

**TOHONO O'ODHAM FEMALE FIGURE, c. 1970**

17.5 x 10; 4 coils/inch, 7 stitches/inch. Close coiled of beargrass foundation with sewing elements of bleached and unbleached yucca and devil's claw. Purchased by the Heard Museum from Byron Hunter's Trading Post, Phoenix, Arizona, NA-SW-PG-B-119

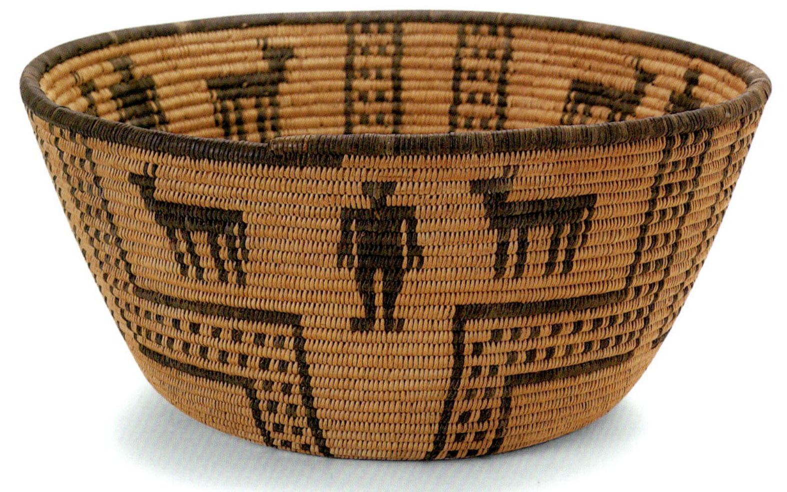

**WESTERN APACHE/YAVAPAI PICTORIAL BASKET, 1900-1920s**

5.5 x 11.75; 5 coils/inch, 15 stitches/inch. Purchased for the original Heard collection in the vicinity of Camp Verde, Arizona, NA-SW-AP-B-1.

*This design of human figures and deer is similar to one woven by a Tohono O'odham elder I know. She saw a photo of an Apache basket in a book and incorporated some of its design elements into her own work, a modern example of how Native basketry traditions have always "cross-pollinated."*

**WESTERN APACHE PICTORIAL OLLA, c. 1920**

19 x 17; 8 coils/inch, 23 stitches/inch. Close coiled three-rod willow foundation with willow and devil's claw sewing elements. Originally in the Bert Robinson Collection, illustrated in *Basketweavers of Arizona* written by Robinson. Gift of Miss Marion R. Plummer and Mr. and Mrs. Stanley W. Plummer, NA-SW-AP-B-246.

*The most impressive thing about this basket is the weaver's ability to keep the vertical lines so straight. As the basket widens and narrows, the lines want to naturally follow along; keeping the "in line" is always a challenge.*

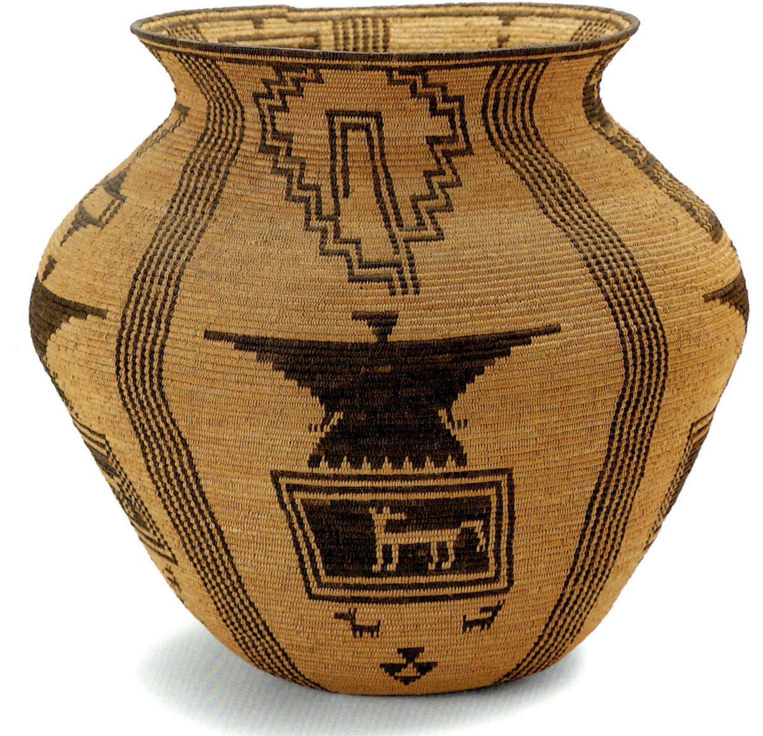

# Ceremony

OR THE TOHONO O'ODHAM— the Desert People—rain is sacred. Every summer, we join together to bring the monsoon rains by "singing down the rain." We spend the hottest weeks of the year collecting the fruit from the tops of the tall saguaro cactus for making the ceremonial wine. We join hands to sing and dance throughout the night, calling to our creator and our animal relations to bring the rain clouds to the desert. Then, as the sun rises, eight young men emerge from the ceremonial house carrying watertight baskets that contain the sacred saguaro fruit wine for the people to drink. And they contain our hopes for rain, for renewal of the desert, for a good new year. In recent years, fewer and fewer of these baskets still exist; sadly, plastic buckets are sometimes used instead. It is heartbreaking to see this happen. Our baskets—not plastic buckets—are sacred. Without them our world is a little less sacred. But it is not too late. Through the Tohono O'odham Basketweavers Organization (TOBO), we are starting to make new wine baskets for the rain ceremony.

The Tohono O'odham are not alone in ceremonial uses for baskets. The pollen, white clay and red clay that are used to paint the face of an Apache girl as she is initiated into womanhood are carried in a special basket. A Hopi bride weaves baskets as gifts for the groom's family. Seri women dance circles around towers of stacked baskets. Whether used to prepare the sacred wine for the Tohono O'odham rain ceremony, to initiate a young woman into a sacred society or as a drum accompaniment to a solemn song, baskets play a rich role in the ceremonial life of Native peoples.

Even in "everyday" baskets, you can see the respect for the sacredness of the world around us. Nature is reflected in so many basketry traditions, from the Wasco school of fish and the Yupik seal to the Hopi butterfly and the Panamint flock of birds. Our world is sacred. So are our baskets.

Today, fewer and fewer baskets are woven for use in the home and in ceremonies. But the spirits of our ancestors still call us to weave the fibers of the land into expressions of beauty and spirit. Throughout the year, I am connected to the cycles of life in the desert. Sharply pointed white yucca is harvested in the heat of the summer; saw-toothed beargrass in the winter; black devil's claw in the garden. I sing for rain and seek the Creator's blessing for a good harvest. As I clean each strand of fiber, my materials begin to speak to me. Their spirit and my dreams combine as I begin to place the first stitches.

Innovation has been a constant thread running through Native basketry traditions. New styles, techniques and materials have always been embraced when they improve utility or enhance beauty. Like the ever-expanding coil of a basket, more and more styles, techniques and visions have become a part of the world of basketry. Just as my elders developed new styles such as split-stitch and horsehair baskets, many weavers today are sharing a new vision of basketry as art.

These personal and cultural expressions of the weaver's vision may no longer serve a "useful" purpose; we now have plastic containers and stainless steel pots. But in many ways these art baskets are the pure expression of a living heritage in which our spirit and creativity are still inspired by the beauty of Creation and the life of our communities.

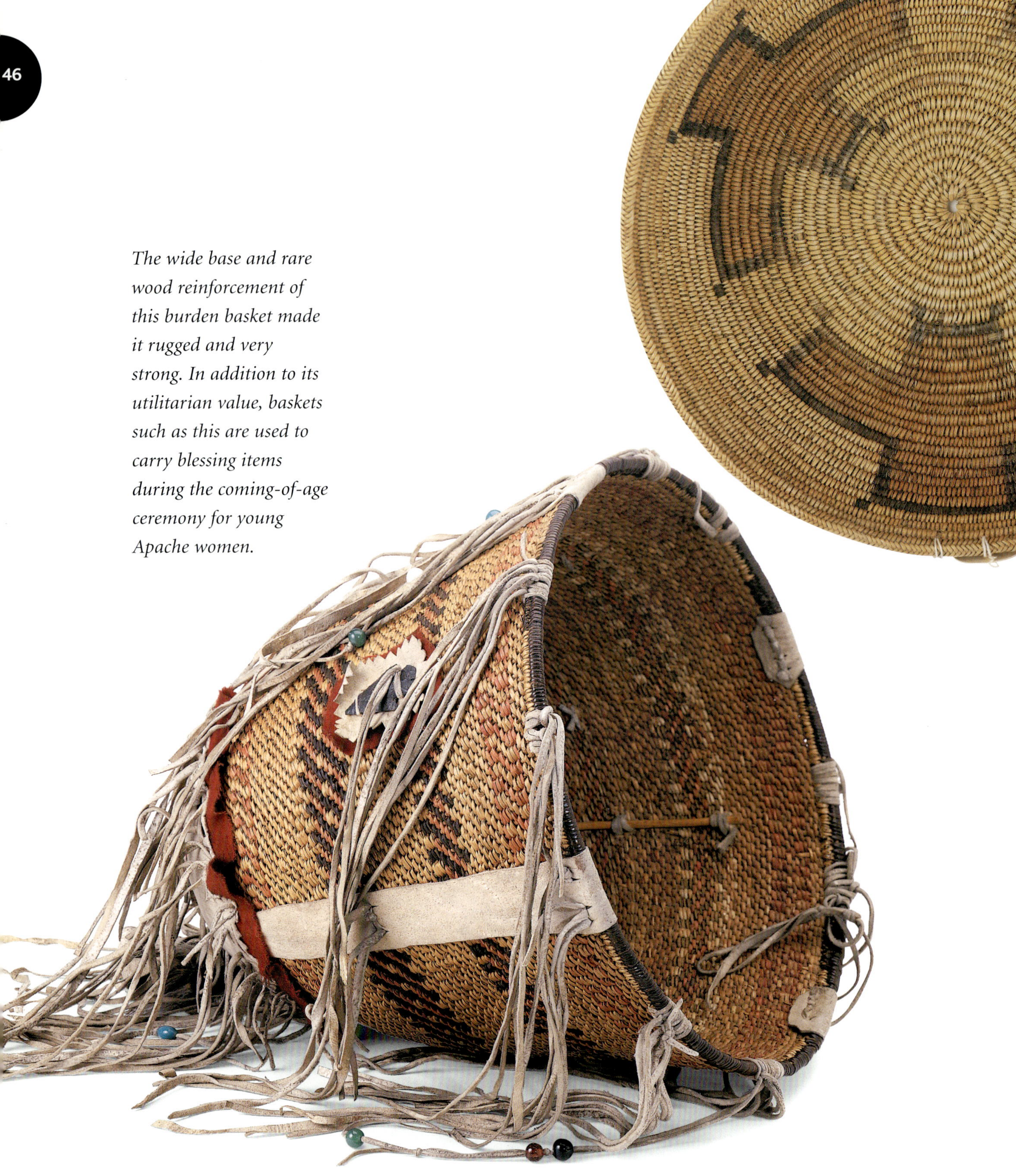

*The wide base and rare wood reinforcement of this burden basket made it rugged and very strong. In addition to its utilitarian value, baskets such as this are used to carry blessing items during the coming-of-age ceremony for young Apache women.*

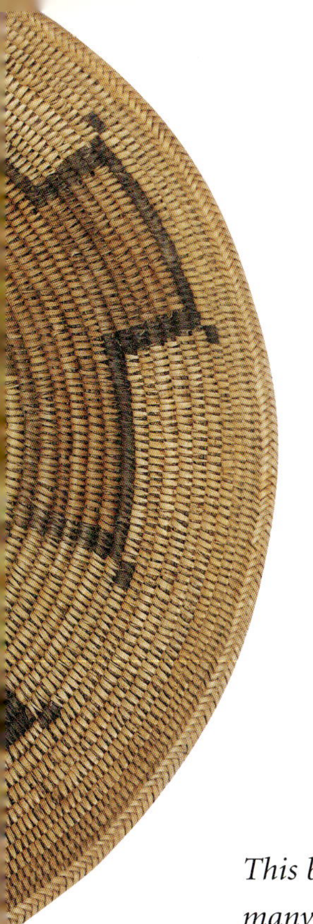



*This basket is sacred to my people. For many years, it held the ceremonial saguaro fruit wine that is a part of our Nawait I'i Rain Ceremony. Without the ceremony, the monsoon rains would not come to our desert homeland. The whirlwind design seems to be calling for the winds that precede the rains to begin blowing. To this day, we join together every summer to "sing down the rain."*

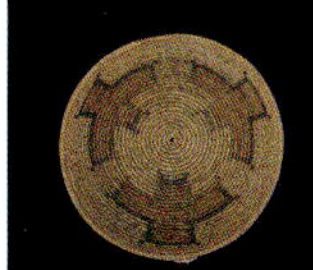

**NAVAJO BOWL BASKET, c. 1900**

3.25 x 12.5; 4 coils/inch, 11 stitches/inch. Close coiled on a two-rod-and-bundle foundation of sumac and yucca fibers with sewing element of sumac dyed with mineral and vegetal dyes; herringbone rim finish. Fred Harvey Fine Arts Collection, 242BA.

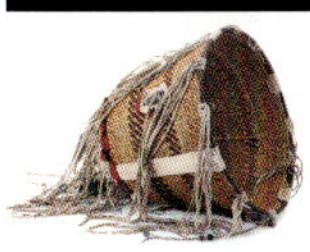

**WESTERN APACHE BURDEN BASKET, c. 1950**

13 x 14.5; 7 warps/inch, 6 wefts/inch. Diagonal and other twilled twining of mulberry, cottonwood or willow and devil's claw, with buckskin, red wool fabric, glass beads, stone projectile points. Gift of Mrs. Barbara Lenone, NA-SW-AP-B-100.

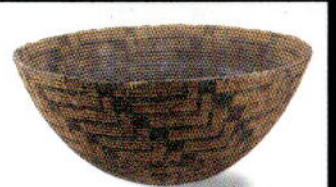

**TOHONO O'ODHAM WINE BASKET, 1900-1930**

9.75 x 20; 4 coils/inch, 9 stitches/inch. Close coiled on a beargrass bundle foundation with willow and devil's claw sewing elements. Acquired by the donors from Al Packard, Santa Fe, New Mexico, in 1971. Gift of Mr. and Mrs. Byron Harvey III, NA-SW-PG-B-67.

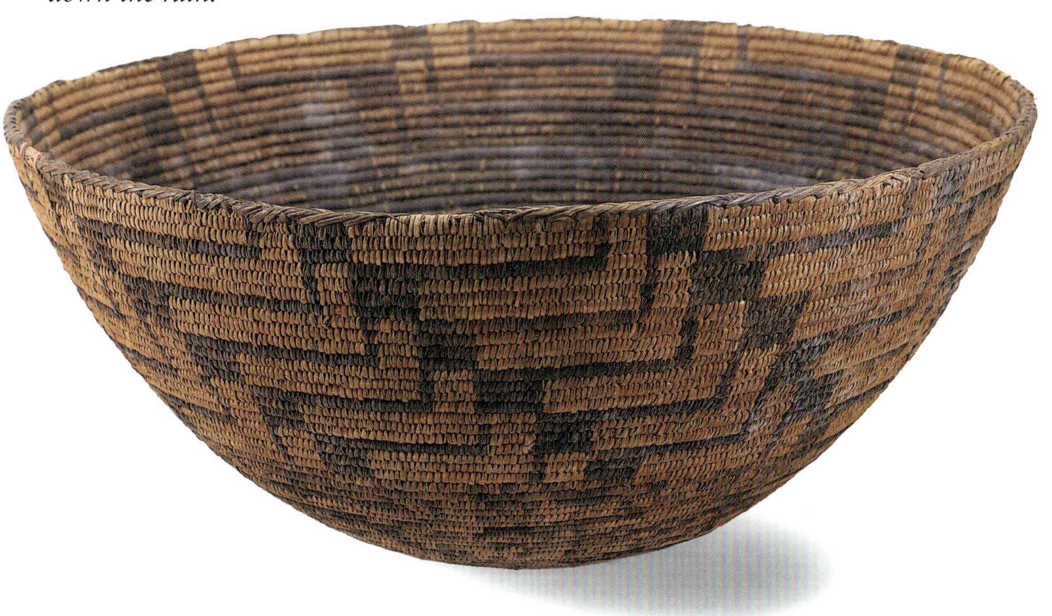

# Artistry

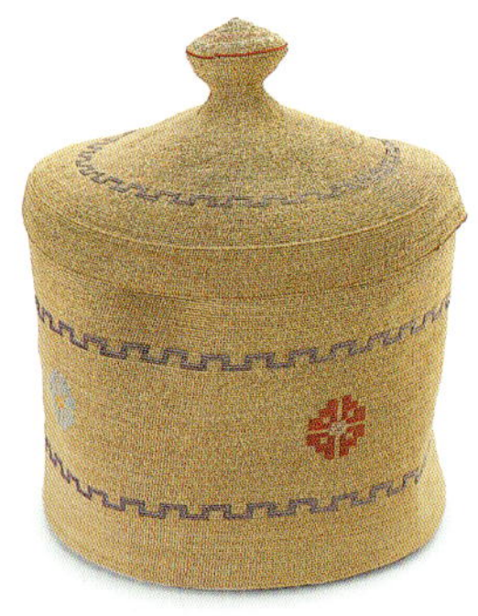

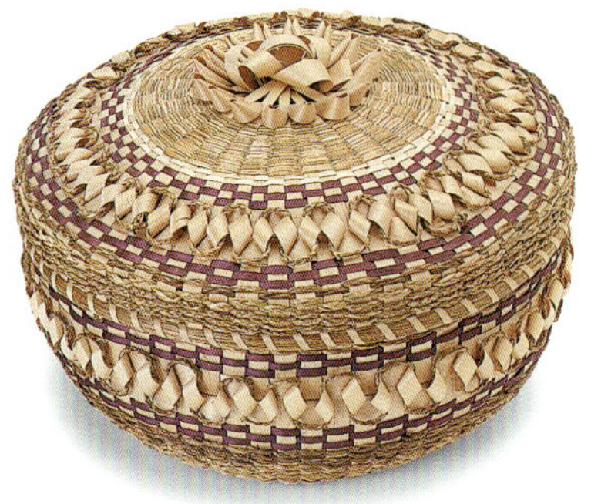

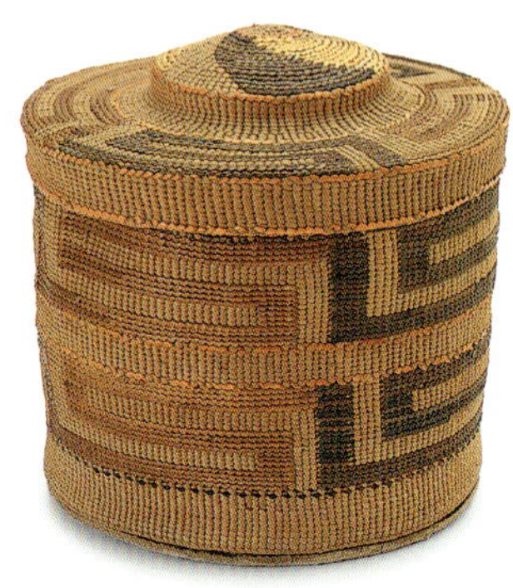

*To weave a basket this fine requires your blood, sweat and tears. The weaver must have used sewing needles that poked her fingers as often as they made holes in the basket. But this commitment made a paper thin—almost cloth-like—basket. The use of embroidery silk in creating this basket more than a century ago shows how weavers have always taken on new challenges, bringing new materials and techniques into their work. Innovation is one of the great traditions of Native lifeways.*

*For me, the use of materials in this basket is amazing. Sweetgrass is such a flexible material; you can braid it or use it as individual fibers. And its wonderful smell returns if it is moistened. You can also see the growth rings of the tree in the ash splints.*

*The hidden secret of this basket is in the handle of the lid—a rattle made from gizzard stones. There are often things that are hidden in baskets, surprises created by the weaver.*

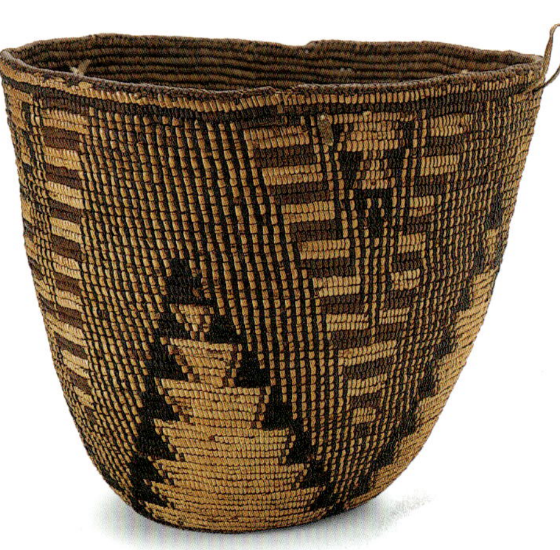

*The use of the imbricated technique makes this basket seem similar to quillwork. It is very complex and time-consuming to do. Looking at the bottom of the basket, I was struck by the red star design there. A weaver who was creating a basket to sit on a shelf to be admired would never have bothered with such a hidden detail. But this basket was meant to be carried around and used; only then could the total design of this basket be fully appreciated.*

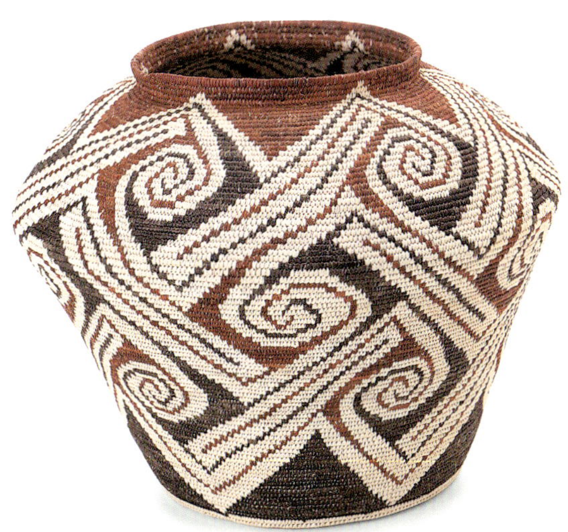

*Annie Antone's work is amazing. So many of her shapes and designs come from ancient Hohokam pottery. The way she incorporates such complex and swirling patterns into basketry is unique and inspiring. She is a great innovator, while still using traditional techniques and materials.*

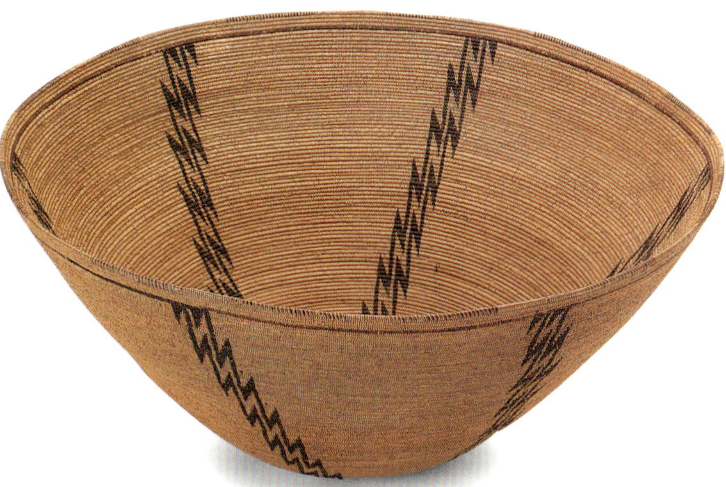

*The beautiful simplicity of the lightning design reflects the strong tie of the weaver to the power of the natural world. It is wonderfully woven, with both the inside and outside equally fine. Yet it contains a deliberate flaw toward the bottom. Maybe the weaver understood that the perfection and beauty of nature could never be matched by human hands.*

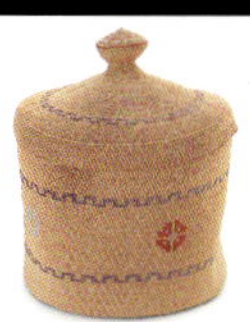

### ALEUT BASKET WITH LID, 1890-1910

5 x 4; 36 warps/inch, 26 wefts/inch. Closed twined rye grass with silk thread false embroidery. Heard Museum Purchase, NA-ES-AL-B-8.

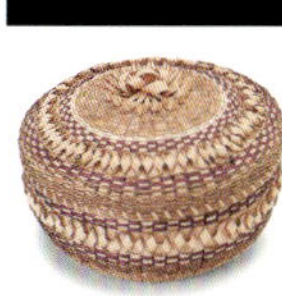

### MARY ADAMS

**Akwesasne Mohawk**

**Basket with lid, 1990**

7.5 x 10.25. Plaited of natural and dyed ash splints and braided sweetgrass. Gift of Dore and Greg McKennis, 3582-1A,B.

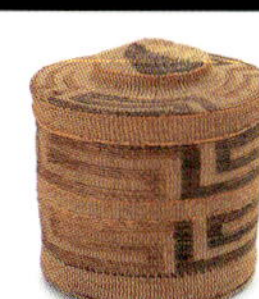

### TLINGIT BASKET WITH RATTLE HANDLE LID, EARLY 1900s

4.5 x 4.75; 14 warps/inch, 20 wefts/inch. Closed twined spruce root with a false embroidery design of aniline dyed beargrass in a wave pattern on the sides and a fern frond design in the center of the lid. Heard Museum Collection, NA-NW-TL-B-42A,B.

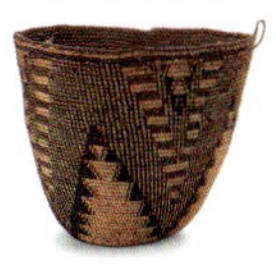

### KLIKITAT BASKET, EARLY 1900

11 x 14; 4 coils/inch, 9 stitches/inch. Close-coiled basket of cedar root with an imbricated design. Gift of Mrs. Barbara Lenone, NA-PT-KL-B-13.

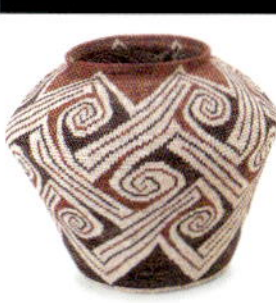

### ANNIE ANTONE

**Tohono O'odham, b. 1955**

**Polychrome olla, 2001**

10.52 x 13.52; 8 coils/inch, 12 stitches/inch. Close coiled on beargrass foundation with sewing elements of yucca, devil's claw and tree yucca root. Purchased from the artist at the Heard Museum Guild Indian Fair and Market, 2001, where the piece received a best of classification award, 4106-1.

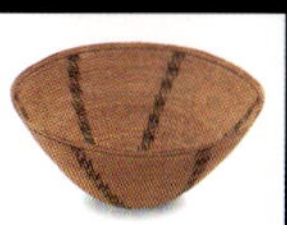

### KITANEMUCK BOWL BASKET. c. 1900

9 x 19.25; 10 coils/inch, 24 stitches/inch. Coiled on a grass bundle foundation with sewing elements of split willow, devil's claw and redbud. Purchased by the Fred Harvey Company in 1910 from the estate of basket collector E.L. McLeod where it, and other baskets from the collection, were featured in Otis T. Mason's *Aboriginal American Basketry,* 138BA.

# Animals + the Natura

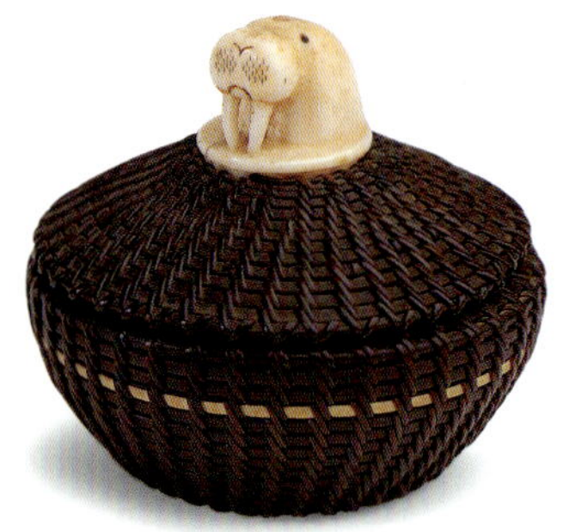

*The tusks of the carving are great, bringing the walrus to life. An Alaskan weaver told me about how hard it is to find white baleen. Working with baleen— cutting it to size—is very difficult.*

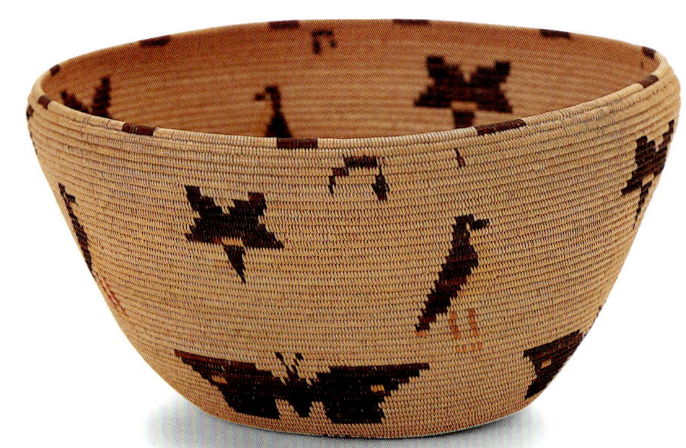

*Even though age has faded this wonderful piece, the weaver used color artfully, giving the birds yellow breasts and brown legs. Details such as this show the ways in which weavers have an intimate knowledge of the animals and plants that share our world.*

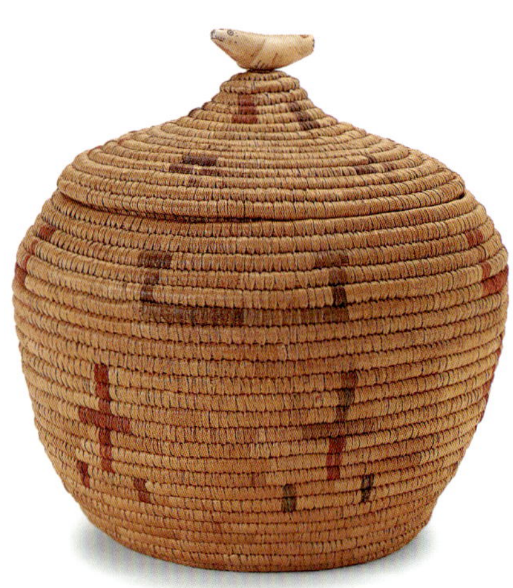

*The personality of the seal is what makes this piece so special. But it is not just added on to the basket as an afterthought. It reminds me of seals I have seen, sunning themselves on rocks with kelp floating around them. There are so many wonderful qualities about this piece that make it inspiring.*

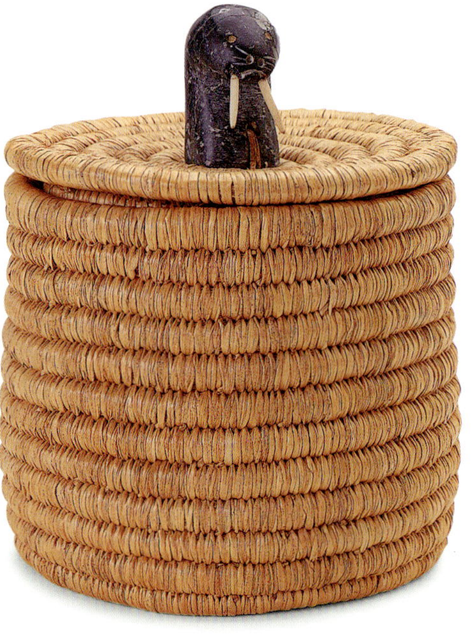

*The seal has a lot of personality and looks like it is raising its head up out of the ocean, with the coils of the basket resembling ripples as the seal's head emerges from the water.*

# World



*The thing that I love about the school of fish on this basket is that each one is slightly different. There are smaller fish and larger fish scattered throughout the design, just as the fish of the seas and rivers also vary. The weaver was closely connected to the natural world, bringing its variety and complexity into her basket.*

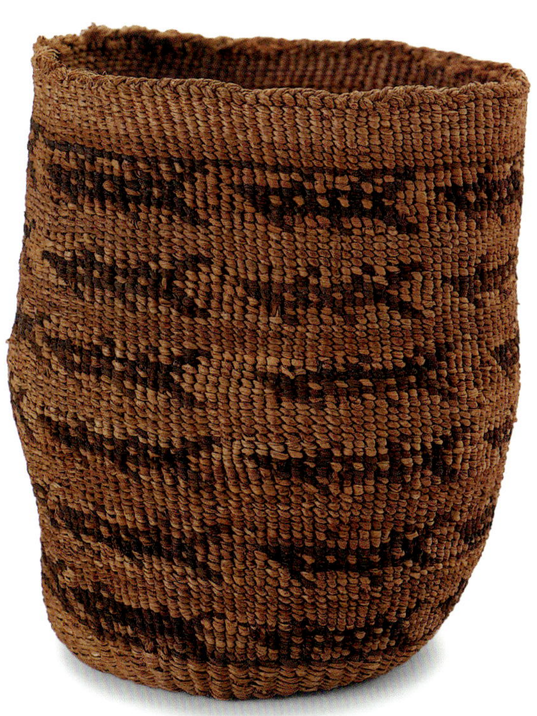

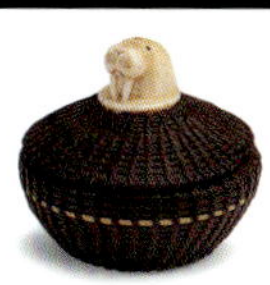

**MARVIN S. PETER**
**Inupiaq, Small Barrow, Alaska**
**Basket with lid, 1949**
2.75 x 3; 10 coils/inch. Open coiled of dark and light baleen with an ivory start on the base that is incised with the number 295 and an ivory walrus head on the lid. Gift of Miss Priscilla Parker, NA-ES-B-29A,B.

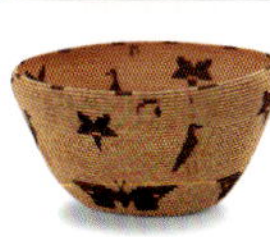

**PANAMINT PICTORIAL BOWL BASKET,**
**c. 1900**
3.52 x 6.75; 12 coils/inch, 30 stitches/inch. Close coiled on a grass foundation with sewing elements of split peeled willow and unpeeled willow, and juncus. Purchased by the Fred Harvey Company from the estate of Las Vegas, Nevada, basket collector Helen Stewart in 1927, 288BA.

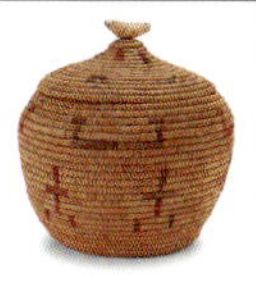

**YUPIK BASKET WITH LID, 1942**
8.5 x 7.75; 4 coils/inch, 8 stitches/inch. Close coiled of rye grass on a bundle foundation, aniline dye, ivory. Gift of Mr. and Mrs. Wilfred Kennel, NA-ES-B-50.

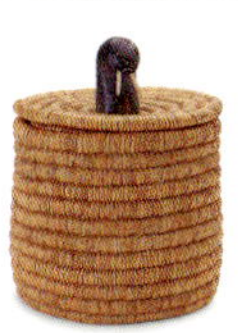

**INUIT BASKET, FROM INUKJOUAK**
**OR "OLD PORT HARRISON"**
**Arctic Quebec basket with carving on lid,**
**1950s**
8.5 x 6.25; 2 coils/inch, 8 stitches/inch. Close coiled of rye grass on a bundle foundation with soapstone and ivory carving. Heard Museum Collection, NA-ES-MIS-B-3.

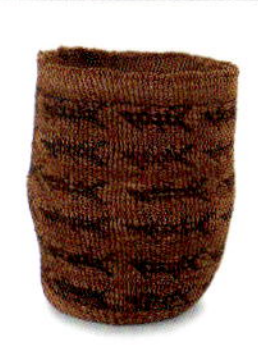

**WASCO/WISHXAM PICTORIAL BASKET,**
**EARLY 1900s**
7.25 x 5.5; 7 warps/inch, 13 wefts/inch. Closed warp twined with warp of two-ply string made of Indian hemp and weft of the same hemp fiber with design in willow bark. Heard Museum Collection, NA-PT-KL-B-8.

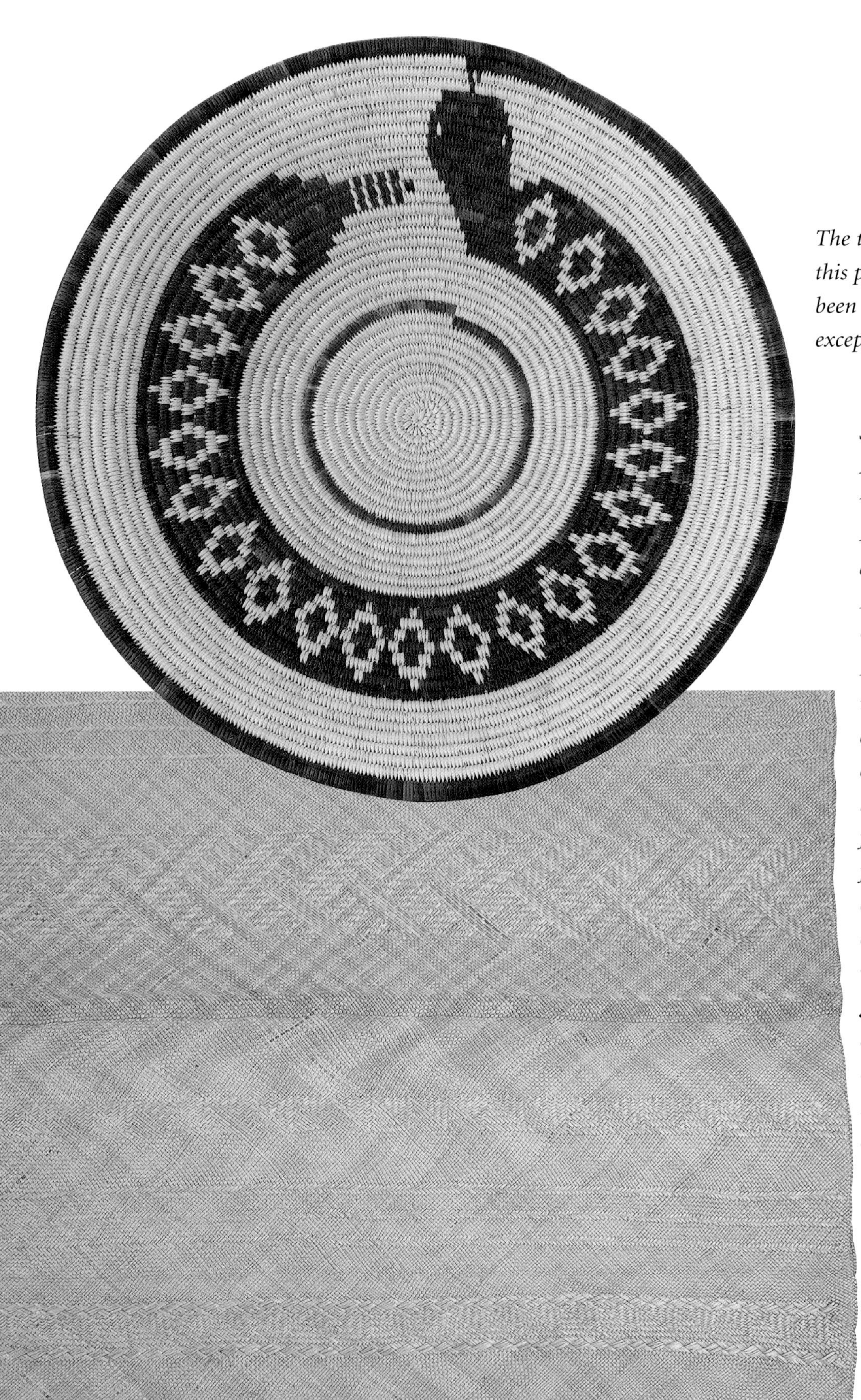

The thick coils on this piece have been pushed down exceptionally well.

Sabra Kauka is a Hawaiian weaver who came to the Heard Museum as an attendee of the Basketweavers Conference and Festival. She identified the mat as one of the finest quality that would have been woven for a chief, either for use as the mat on which he slept or as a floor mat. It would be the finest gift you could give a chief. In the center is the ke'eke'e or wave design composed of chevrons.

**LEROY FISHER**
**Chemehuevi**
**Pictorial basket, 1985**

3.75 x 16; 4 coils/inch, 13 stitches/inch. Close coiled of three-rod foundation with cottonwood and devil's claw sewing elements. Purchased by the Heard Museum from the weaver, NA-SW-CM-B-40.

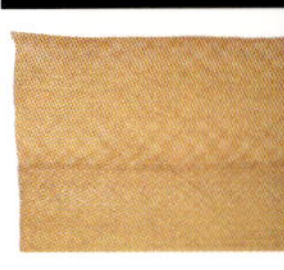

**NI'IHAU, HAWAI'I MAT, 1800s**

73 x 77; 9 elements/inch. Plaited of makaloa sedge, a fresh-water plant. Probably collected in 1924 by Maie Heard, 3280-183.

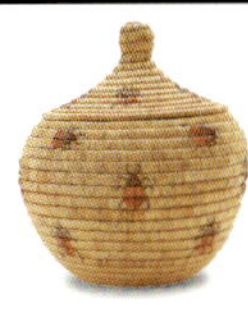

**JULIE A. SIMONS**
**Inuit, possibly Nunivak Island**
**Pictorial basket, 1971**

10.25; 9.5; 2 coils/inch, 11 stitches/inch. Close coiled of rye grass on a bundle foundation, aniline dye. The artist entered this in the Heard Museum Guild Indian Arts and Crafts Exhibit, 1971, where it received an honorable mention ribbon. Purchased by the Heard Museum from the exhibit, NA-ES-MIS-B-2.

*This is one of the most inspiring designs in the show for me. The weaver split the coils—using two different colors of material in this same location on the coil—to create more rounded shapes than would not have been possible using conventional coiling techniques. This opens the door to so many more designs that are floating around in my head. The design is not elaborate on this basket, but it has a big impact both aesthetically and on me as a weaver.*

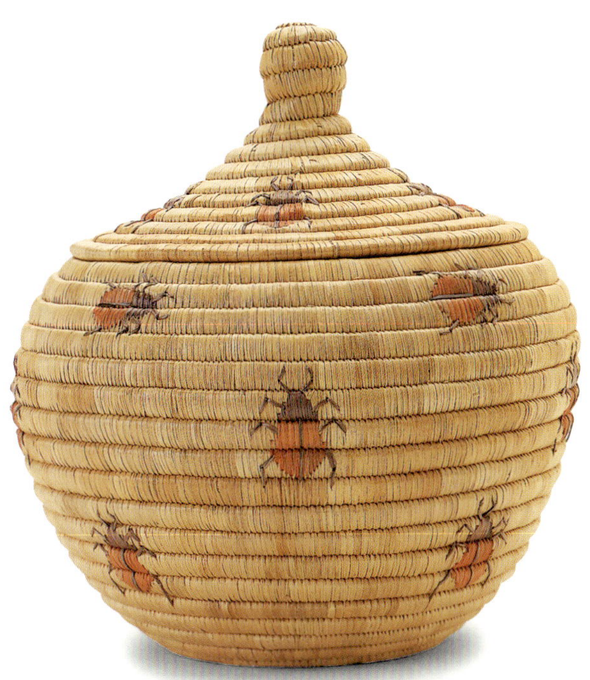

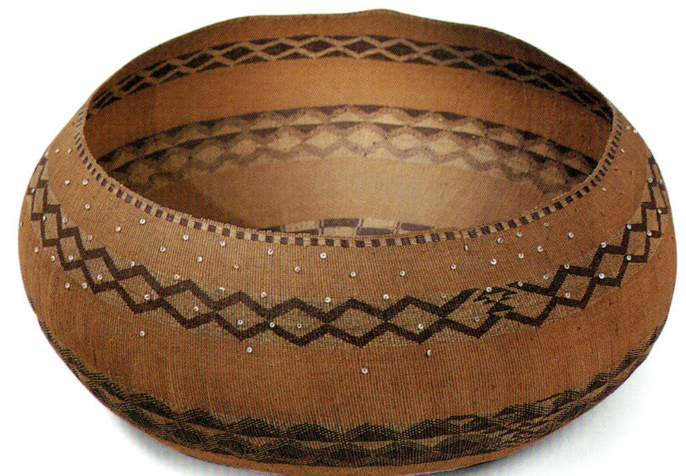

*The simplicity of the design works on this piece. It is attributed to Mary Benson before her "art basket" days. Its beauty challenges that definition of art and makes me question the concept of fine art. I guess the only thing that makes a basket an art basket is when it is not woven for use, because this is clearly a work of art.*

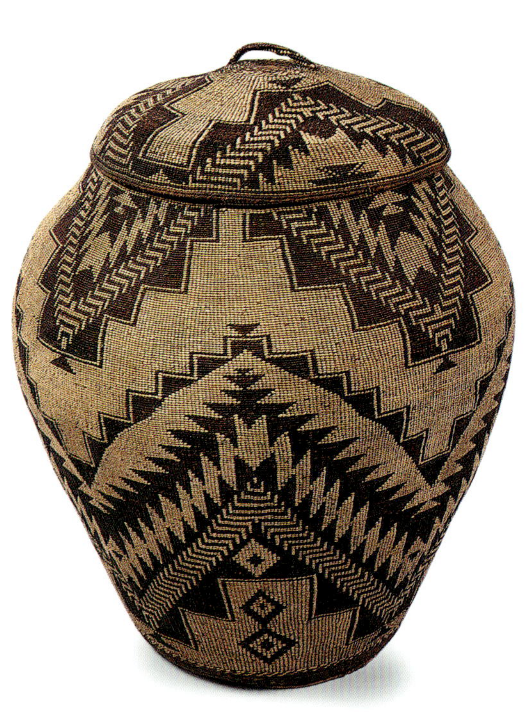

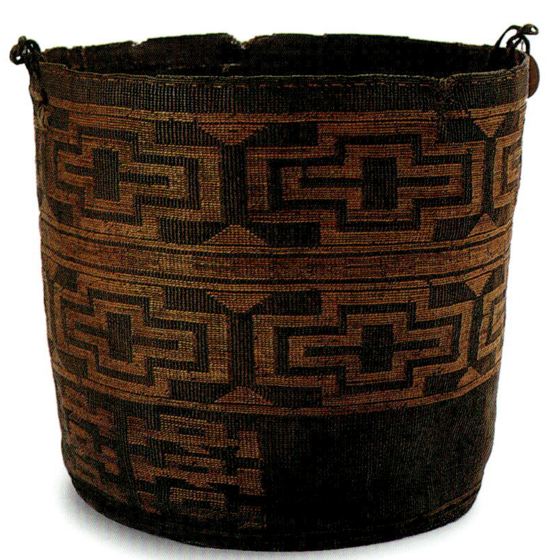

*When I think of this basket being built from scratch and decorated with false embroidery, I am amazed. When I see the color that has come to the basket through the aging process, it reminds me of a person. As we each age, our life is colored by our experiences.*

*This basket is an inspiration to me. It is wonderfully complex and detailed. To do that on such a large scale is impressive.*

# Complexity +

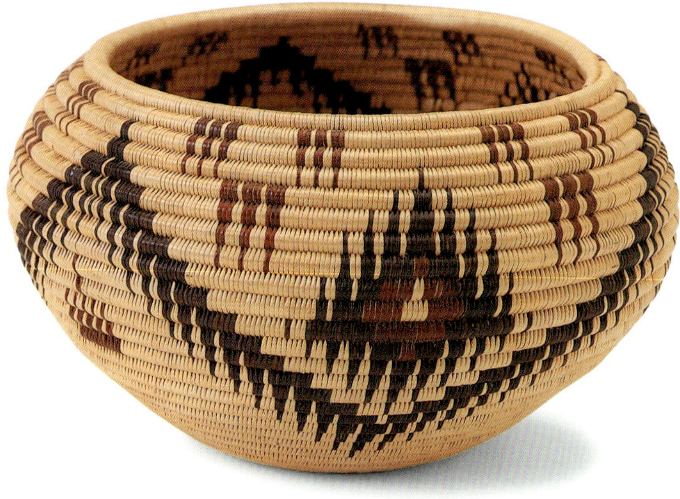

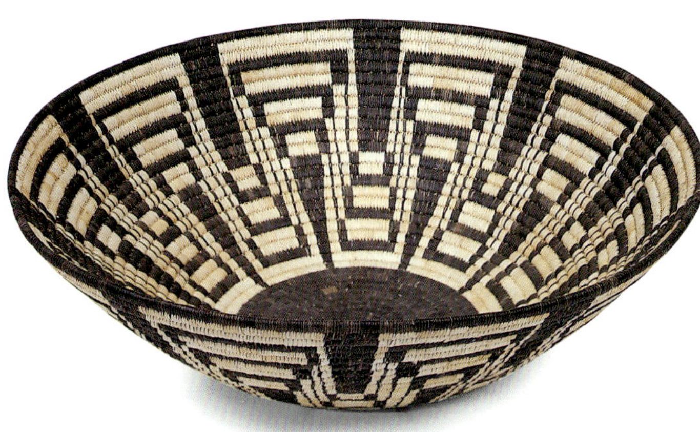



# Simplicity

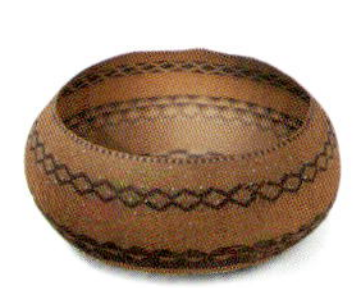

**MARY BENSON**
Pomo
**Basket, c. 1900**

16 x 36; 7 warps/inch, 10 wefts/inch. Closed twined of split pine root with redbud design, ornamented with clam shell disc beads. Acquired by the Fred Harvey Company from the Comstock collection, 53BA.

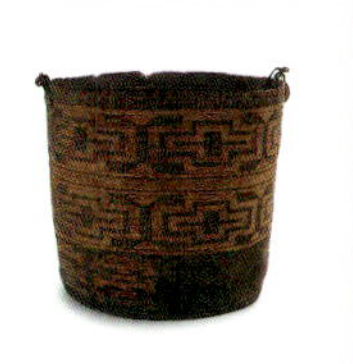

**TLINGIT BASKET, c. 1850**

12.5 x 15; 11 warps/inch, 17 wefts/inch. Closed twined of spruce root with a false embroidery design in beargrass; rawhide handles attached at the interior top. Fred Harvey Fine Arts Collection, 15BA.

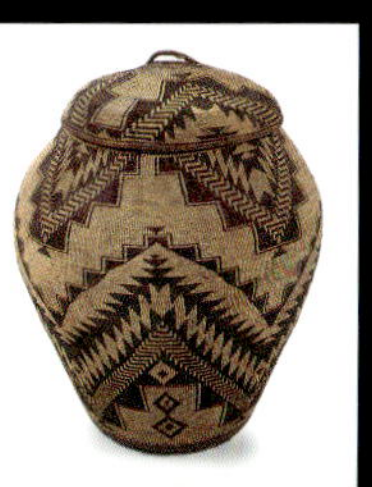

**SHASTA JAR BASKET, LATE 1800s**

31.5 x 15; 6 warps/inch, 8 wefts/inch. Full-twist overlay twining with traditional materials willow stem warps and wefts of pine root or tule root; designs of beargrass and maidenhair fern. Fred Harvey Fine Arts Collection, 818BA.

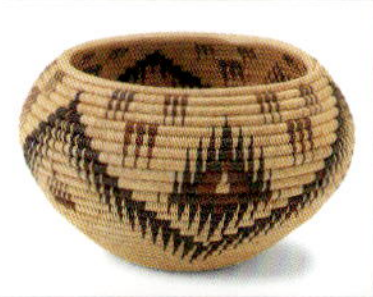

**WASHOE DEGIKUP, EARLY 1900s**

8.5 x 5.25; 4 coils/inch, 18 stitches/inch. Close coiled on a three-rod willow foundation with sewing elements of willow and design in redbud and bracken fern root. Purchased by Herb BraMé for Maie Heard from Cohn's Baskets, The Emporium, Carson City, Nevada, NA-BS-WA-B-7.

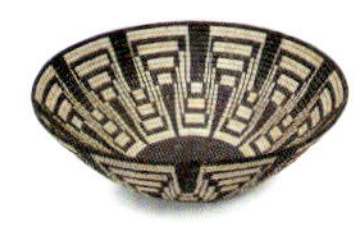

**DOROTHY LOPEZ**
Tohono O'odham
**Squash blossom basket, 1976**

10 x 30; 2 coils/inch, 6 stitches/inch. Close coiled on a beargrass foundation with sewing elements of bleached yucca and devil's claw. Acquired by the donors at the Santa Rosa Trading Post, Sells, Arizona. Gift of Mr. and Mrs. Glenn E. Quick, Sr., NA-SW-PG-B-124.

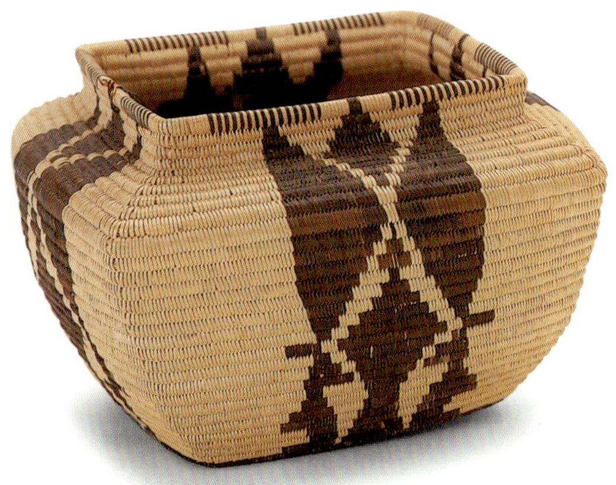

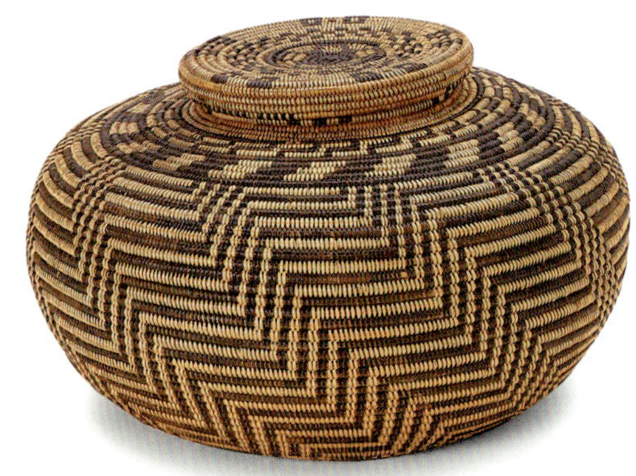

*The perfect shape of this basket makes it a true masterwork. To make such sharp corners is very hard to do well. When I try to make square baskets, they end up kind of round. This weaver showed tremendous skill and control in weaving this form.*

*This pattern reminds me of the whirlwind design used by Tohono O'odham weavers. And the use of juncus in the neck is impressive because it is such a difficult material to work with.*

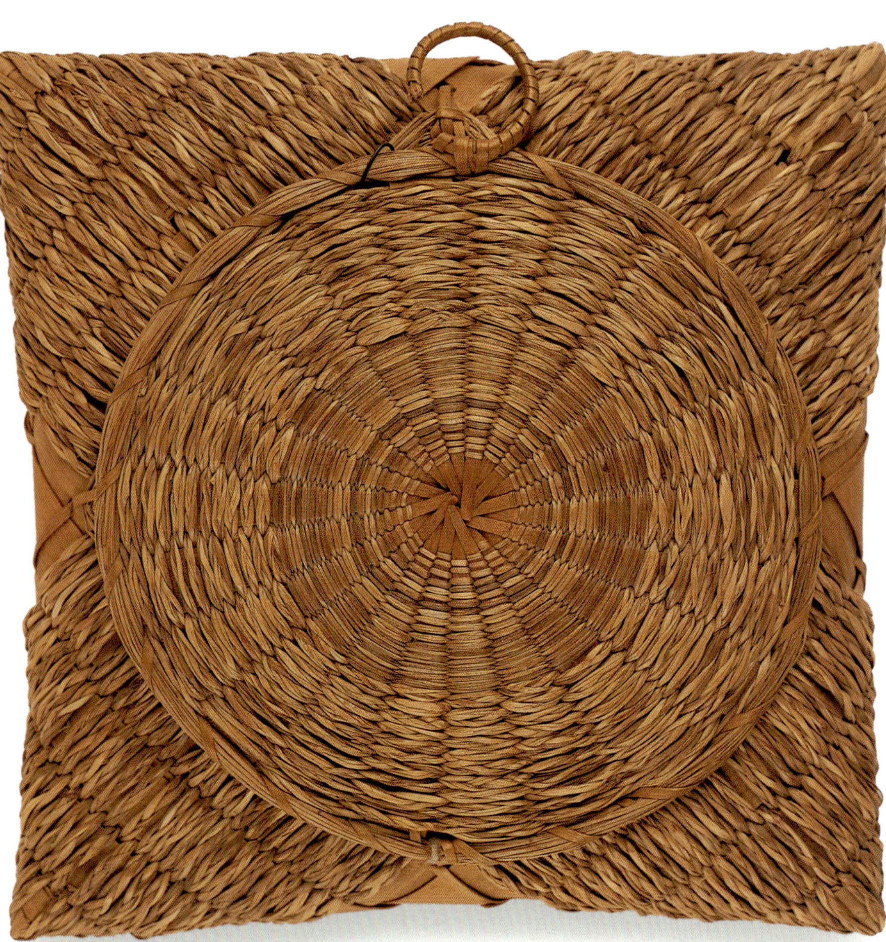

*The combination of square and round shapes in this basket makes it special.*

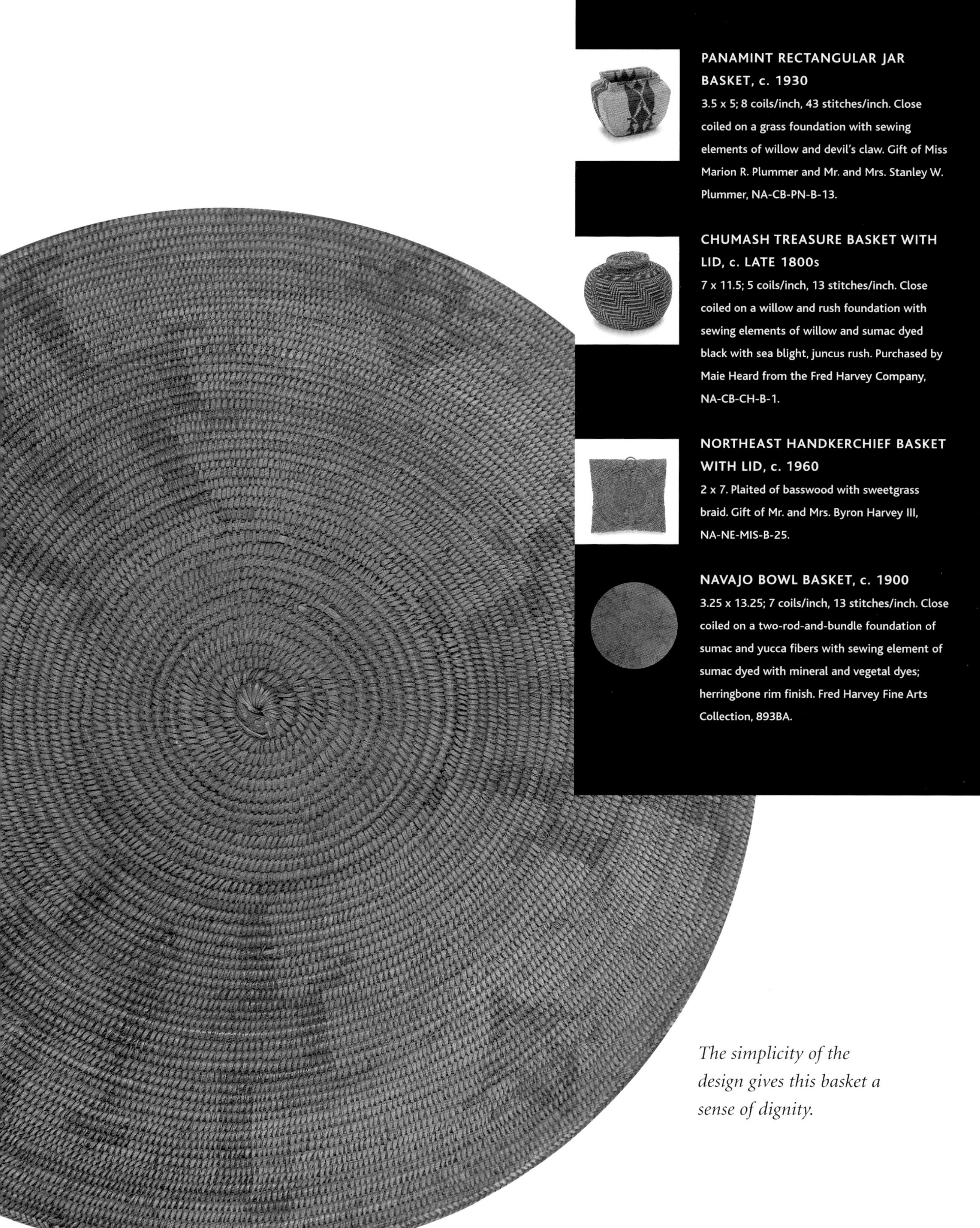

## PANAMINT RECTANGULAR JAR BASKET, c. 1930

3.5 x 5; 8 coils/inch, 43 stitches/inch. Close coiled on a grass foundation with sewing elements of willow and devil's claw. Gift of Miss Marion R. Plummer and Mr. and Mrs. Stanley W. Plummer, NA-CB-PN-B-13.

## CHUMASH TREASURE BASKET WITH LID, c. LATE 1800s

7 x 11.5; 5 coils/inch, 13 stitches/inch. Close coiled on a willow and rush foundation with sewing elements of willow and sumac dyed black with sea blight, juncus rush. Purchased by Maie Heard from the Fred Harvey Company, NA-CB-CH-B-1.

## NORTHEAST HANDKERCHIEF BASKET WITH LID, c. 1960

2 x 7. Plaited of basswood with sweetgrass braid. Gift of Mr. and Mrs. Byron Harvey III, NA-NE-MIS-B-25.

## NAVAJO BOWL BASKET, c. 1900

3.25 x 13.25; 7 coils/inch, 13 stitches/inch. Close coiled on a two-rod-and-bundle foundation of sumac and yucca fibers with sewing element of sumac dyed with mineral and vegetal dyes; herringbone rim finish. Fred Harvey Fine Arts Collection, 893BA.

*The simplicity of the design gives this basket a sense of dignity.*

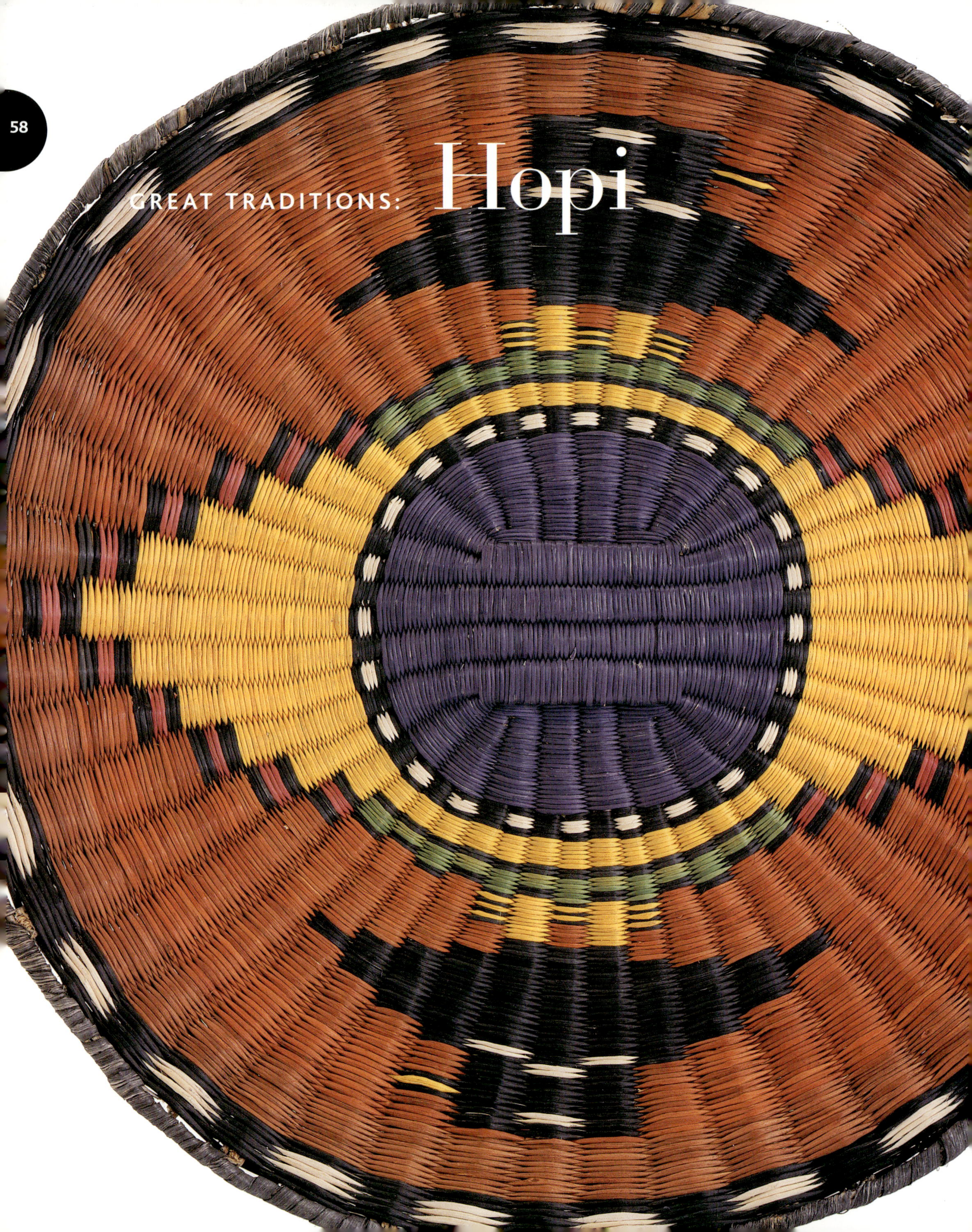

58
GREAT TRADITIONS: Hopi

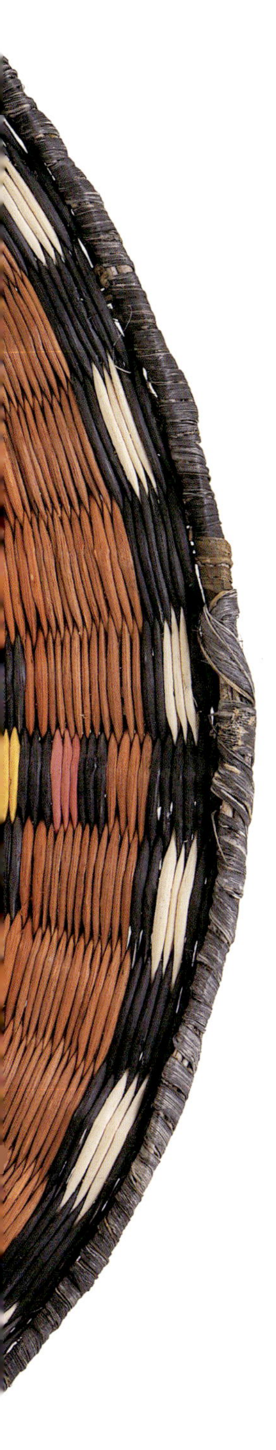

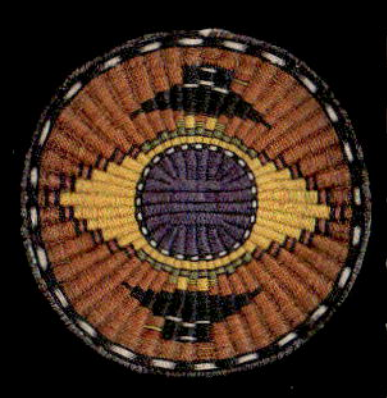

**HOPI, THIRD MESA PICTORIAL PLAQUE, 1970**

.5 x 14.5; 13 wefts/inch. Wicker with dunebroom warps and rabbitbrush wefts with aniline dyes, yucca wrap at rim. Gift of Mr. and Mrs. Byron Harvey III, NA-SW-HO-B-152.

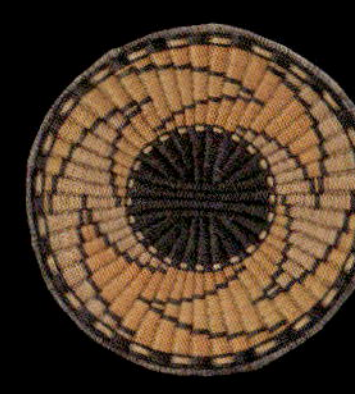

**HOPI, THIRD MESA BASKETRY PLAQUE, c. 1925**

.5 x 13; 16 wefts/inch. Wicker with dunebroom warps and aniline dyed rabbitbrush. Gift of Mr. B. P. O'Sullivan and Mrs. Natalie O'Sullivan, NA-SW-HO-B-394.

*Working with wicker requires lots of strength. Pushing the wefts down and pulling them tight is hard work.*

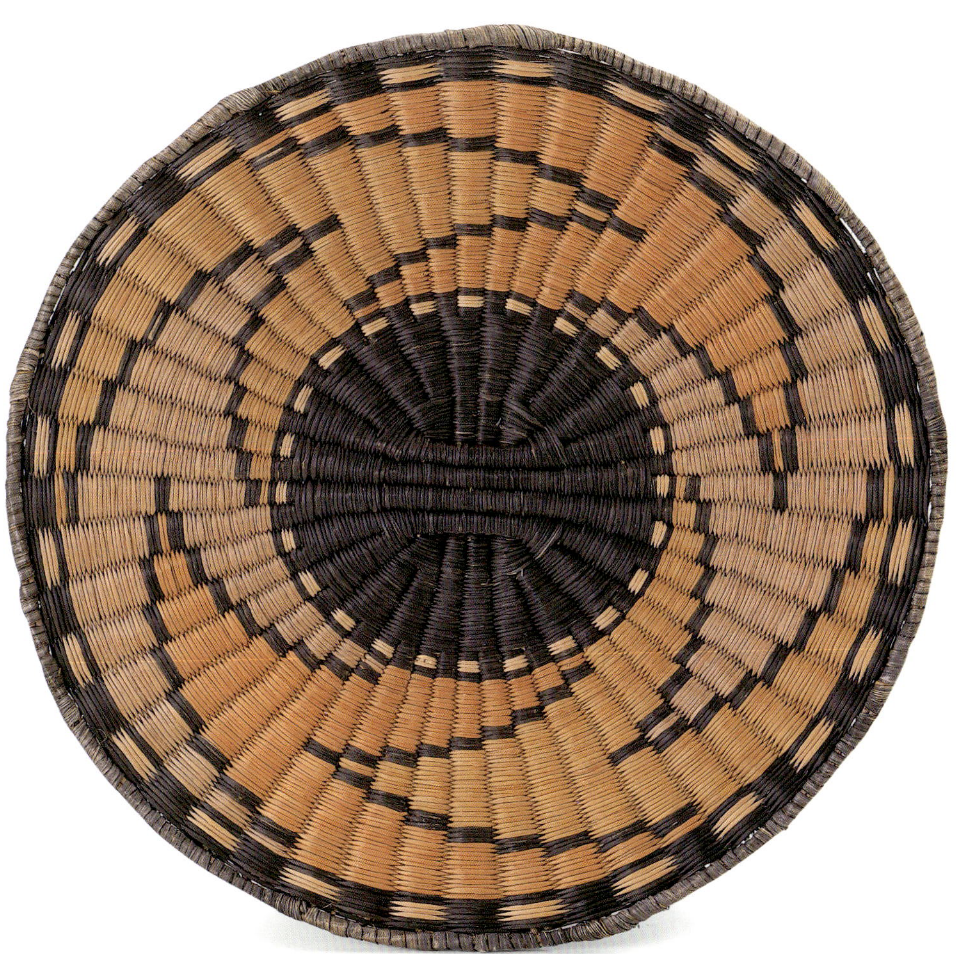

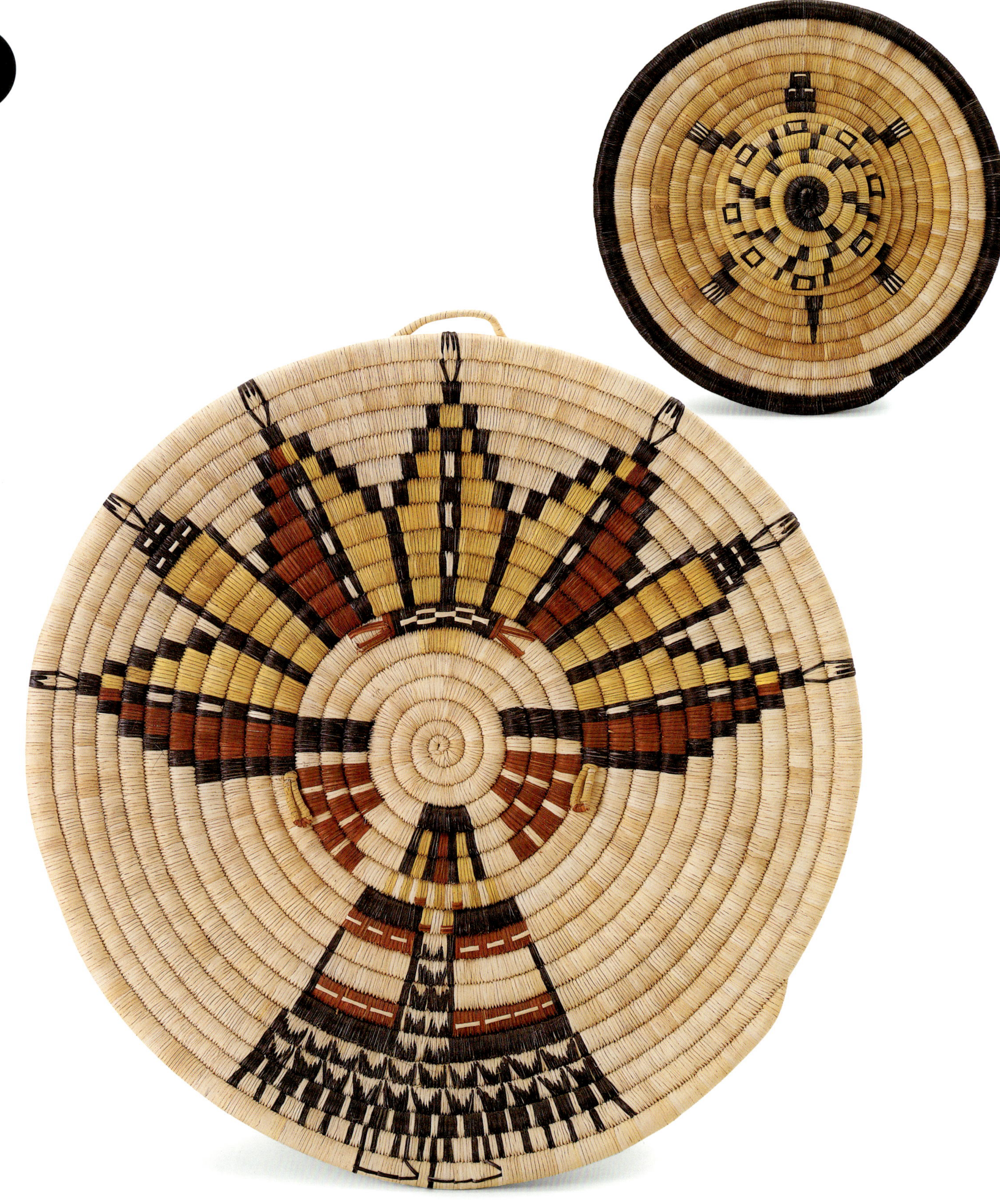

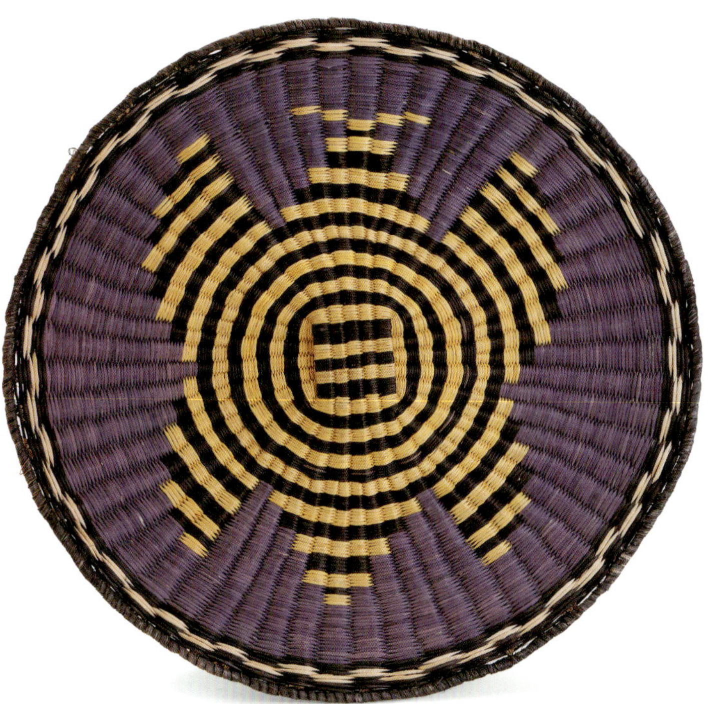

*The clean stripes of the butterfly in this basket make it striking.*

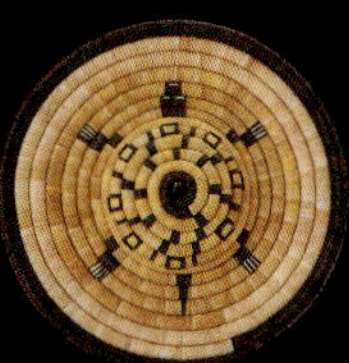

### HOPI, SECOND MESA PICTORIAL PLAQUE, 1969

2 x 10; 13 wefts/inch. Close coiled with a bundle foundation of galleta grass with sewing elements of bleached and unbleached yucca and aniline dyes. Gift of Mr. and Mrs. Byron Harvey III, NA-SW-HO-B-176.

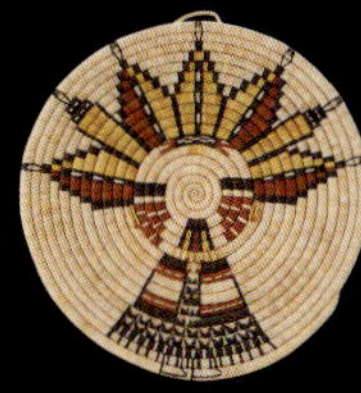

### HOPI, SECOND MESA PICTORIAL PLAQUE, FEMALE SA'LAKO, 1970

.5 x 14: 2.5 coils/inch, 18 stitches/inch. Close coiled with bundle foundation of galleta grass and sewing elements of bleached and dyed yucca, with decorative stitches in the beading technique and raised coils to denote hair. Gift of Mr. and Mrs. Byron Harvey III, NA-SW-HO-B-75.

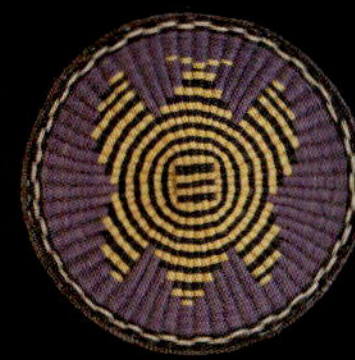

### HOPI, THIRD MESA PICTORIAL PLAQUE, 1970

.5 x 14; 2.5 wefts/inch. Wicker with dunebroom warps and rabbitbrush wefts with aniline dyes, yucca wrap at rim. Gift of Mr. and Mrs. Byron Harvey III, NA-SW-HO-B-129.

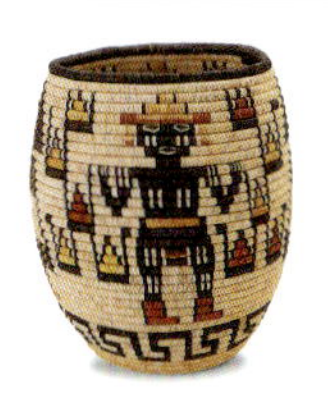

### ALBERTA SUSUNKEWA
**Hopi, Second Mesa**
**Pictorial basket of Crow Mother and P'qang'hoya with rain clouds, 1974**
13 x 8.5; 2.5 coils/inch, 17 stitches/inch. Close coiled with a bundle foundation of galleta grass with sewing elements of bleached and unbleached yucca, and dyed elements. This basket won a second prize at a Museum of Northern Arizona Hopi Show, Flagstaff. Heard Museum Purchase, NA-SW-HO-B-293.

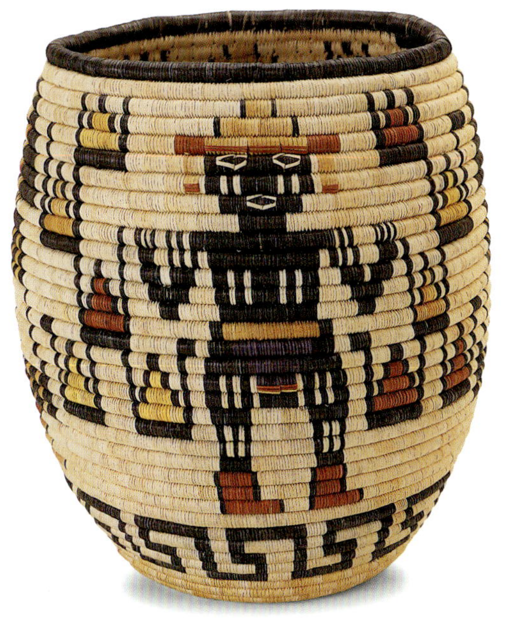

*This wonderful piece makes my hands hurt just thinking about it. To work with a large coil like this takes a lot of strength. Weavers work with all of their senses to create a work like this. Of course, we use our eyes. But we also use our hands to feel for evenness. We smell the materials to tell if they are fresh or if they have gone bad. And we use our "sixth sense" to inspire us.*

 # Pomo

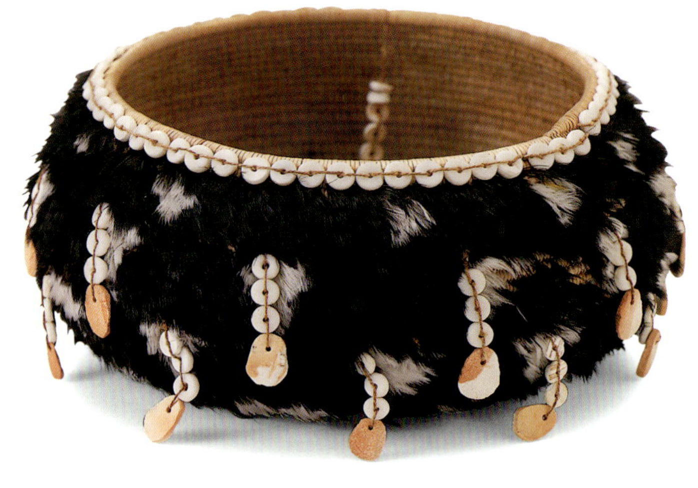

*As the piece moves, the light causes the iridescent materials—both feathers and abalone—to change. The weaver's selection of iridescent materials is the strength of the piece. To me, this basket is all about light. The feathers change color and reflect light at different angles. They are complemented by the iridescence of the abalone shell.*

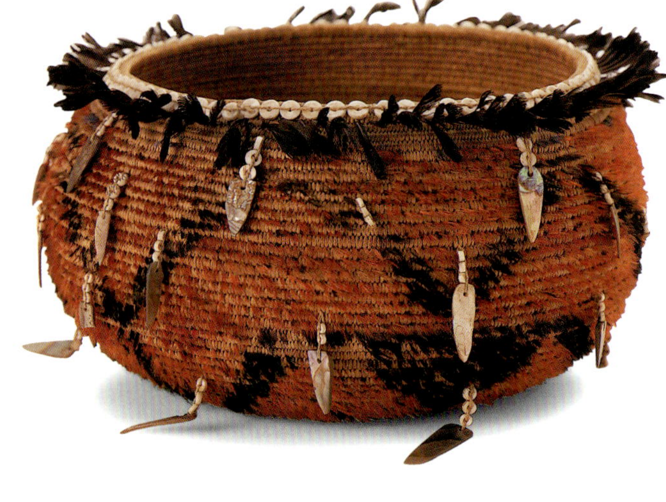

*When it was first made, this basket must have been even more vibrant and bright. When I first wove baskets with pendants similar to these, I thought that I was being innovative. Only later did I learn that weavers have done this for generations. Sometimes the same artistic vision comes to more than one person. I guess the creative spirit inspires us and carries lessons from the past to us in our dreams.*

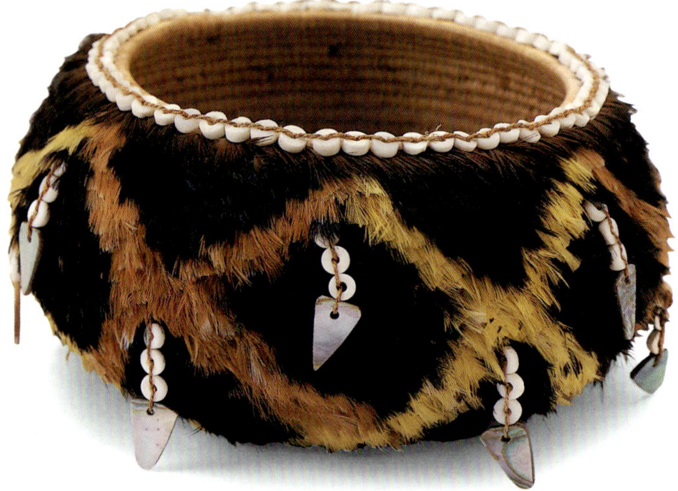

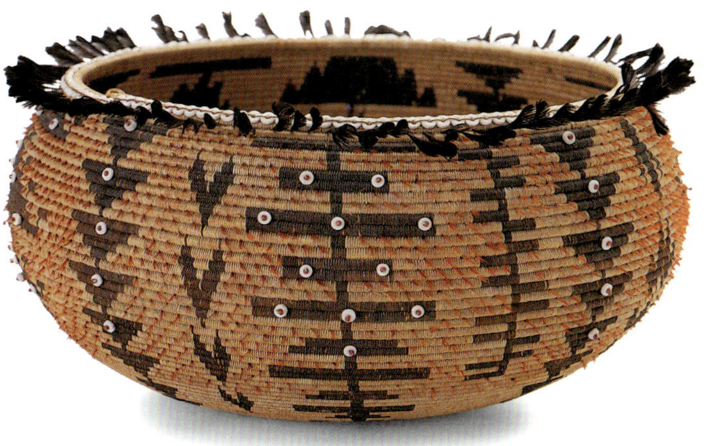

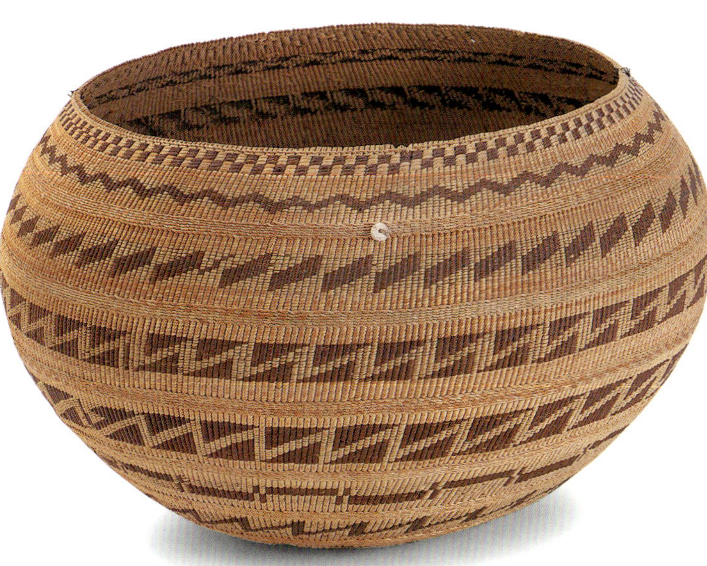

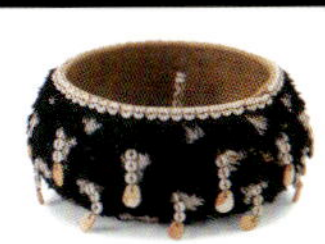

### POMO FEATHERED GIFT BASKET, c. 1900

3 x 6.5; 8 coils/inch, 22 stitches/inch. Coiled on a willow foundation with sewing material of sedge grass root with Bullock oriole and Lake grebe feathers. Orange beads are magnesite baked in a reducing atmosphere. Fred Harvey Fine Arts Collection, 519BA.

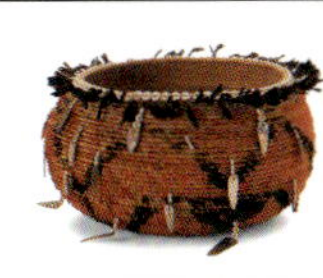

### POMO GIFT BASKET, 1919

4.75 x 8.5; 8 coils/inch, 22 stitches/inch. Close coiled on a three rod willow foundation with a sedge root weft, clam shell disc beads, abalone pendants and feathers including quail top knots, red woodpecker, green mallard duck, bluebird, unidentified white and brown feathers. Gift of Mr. and Mrs. Henry S. Galbraith, 3309-225.

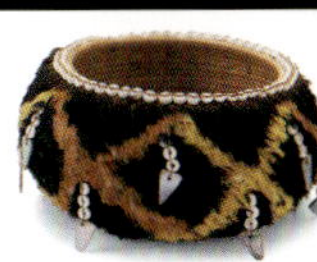

### POMO FEATHERED GIFT BASKET, c. 1900

2.5 x 5; 8 coils/inch, 30 stitches/inch. Coiled on a willow foundation with sewing material of sedge root; feathers of mallard duck, pigeon, Baltimore oriole, robin, clam shell disc beads with abalone pendants. Fred Harvey Fine Arts Collection, 523BA.

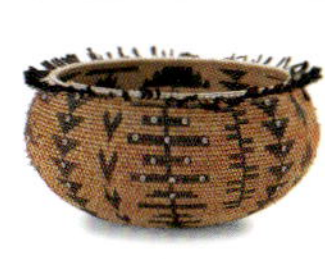

### ALICE WORRIS
#### Pomo, c. 1845-1914
#### Feathered wedding basket, c. 1900

6 x 10.5; 9 coils/inch, 28 stitches/inch. Coiled on a three-rod willow foundation with sewing elements of sedge root and dyed bulrush root, ornamented with clam shell beads and red seed beads sewn on with native twine and with quail plumes. Maker attribution by Sally McLendon, Hunter College and City University of New York. Fred Harvey Fine Arts Collection, 525BA.

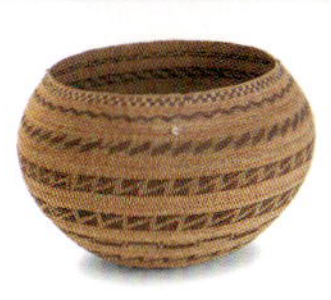

### MARY OR WILLIAM BENSON
#### Pomo
#### Basket, 1904

9.5 x 14; 9 warps/inch, 12 wefts/inch. Full-twist twined and three-strand twining with willow warps and wefts of sedge and redbud root. Fred Harvey Fine Arts Collection, 844BA.

# O'odham

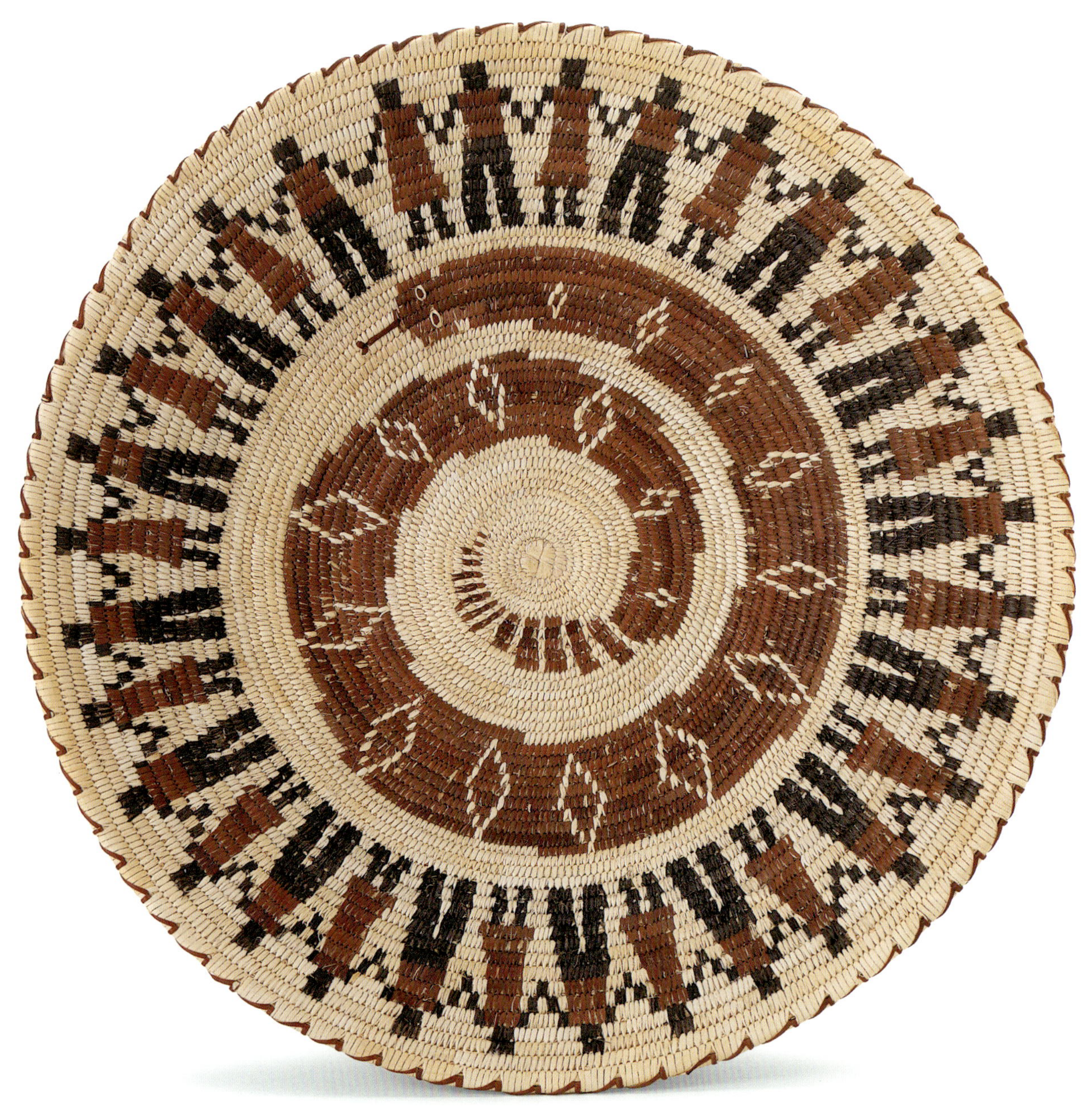

*Mary Thomas is well known for her miniature baskets. With such a fine coil, this is like a huge miniature. The people around the rim hold hands for the friendship dance. Engaging in such dances and singing traditional songs is a central part of my cultural tradition.*

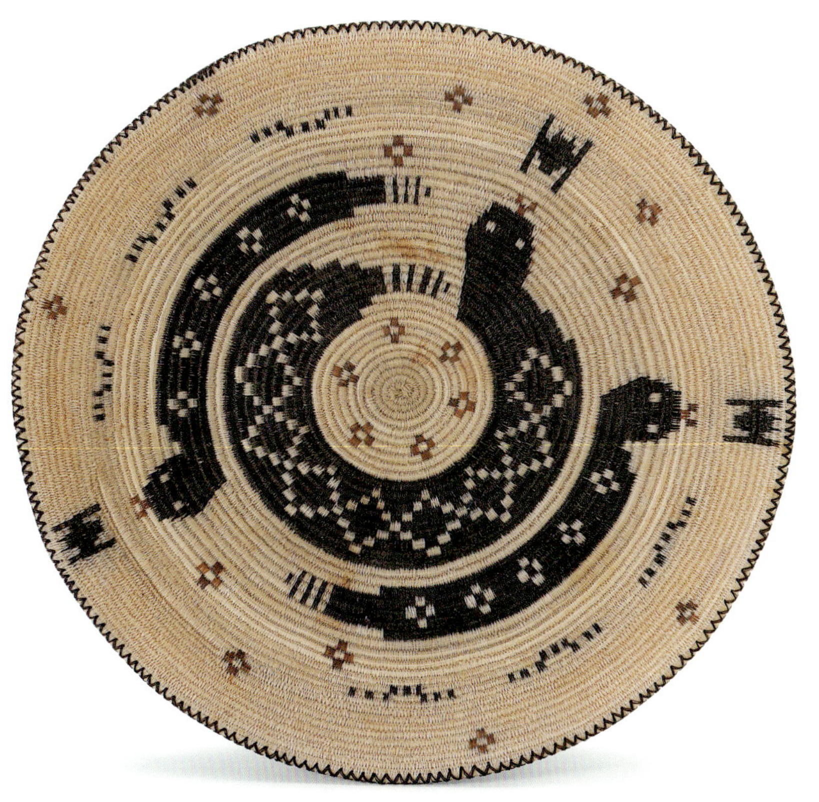

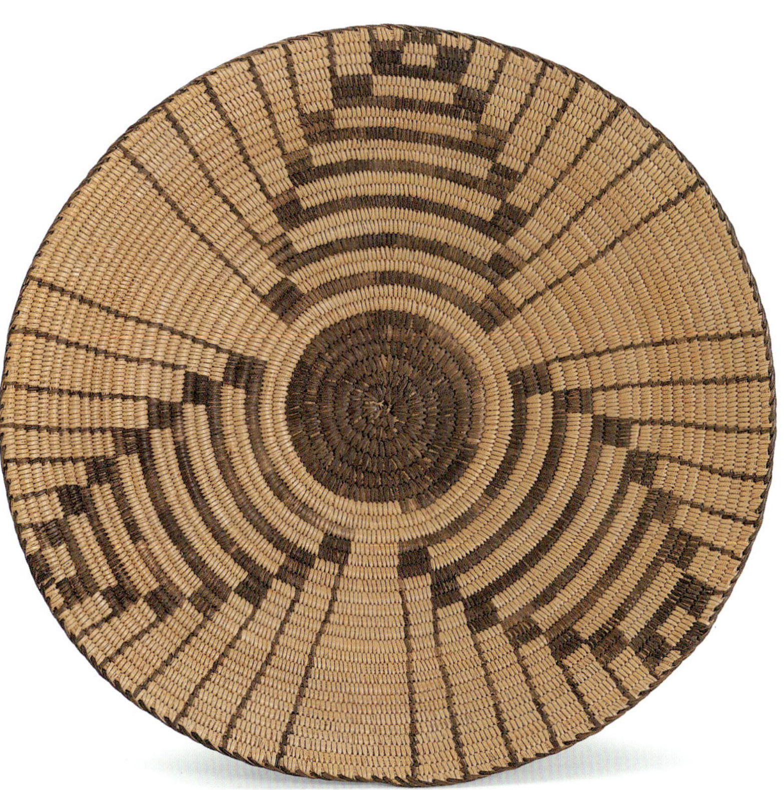

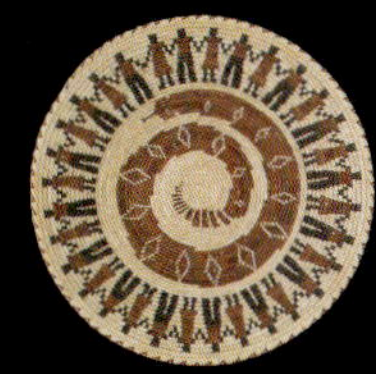

**MARY THOMAS**
Tohono O'odham
Friendship basket, 1981
2 x 10.5; 9 coils/inch, 16 stitches/inch.
Close coiled of beargrass foundation with sewing elements of bleached yucca, tree yucca root and devil's claw. Purchased by Mrs. Mary Coughlin for the museum collection from the Heard Museum Guild Native American Arts Show of 1981, NA-SW-PG-B-200.

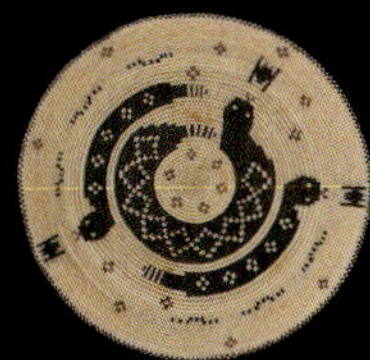

**TOHONO O'ODHAM PICTORIAL BASKET, 1970s**
.5 x 8.75; 12 coils/inch, 32 stitches/inch.
Close coiled of horsehair. Gift of Mr. Michael Mulberger, NA-SW-PG-B-187.

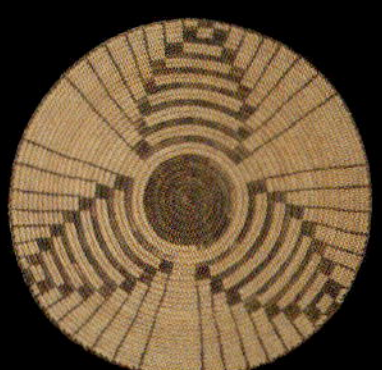

**AKIMEL O'ODHAM THREE-PETAL SQUASH BLOSSOM BASKET, EARLY 1900s**
.25 x 9.25; 7 coils/inch, 16 stitches/inch.
Close coiled with a cattail bundle foundation and willow and devil's claw. Purchased by Maie Heard for the original museum collection, NA-SW-PI-B-11.

*The stitching on the three-petal squash blossom is amazing. It is so uniform and fine that you cannot tell the difference between the front and the back. That is very hard to do.*

# GREAT TRADITIONS: Panamint

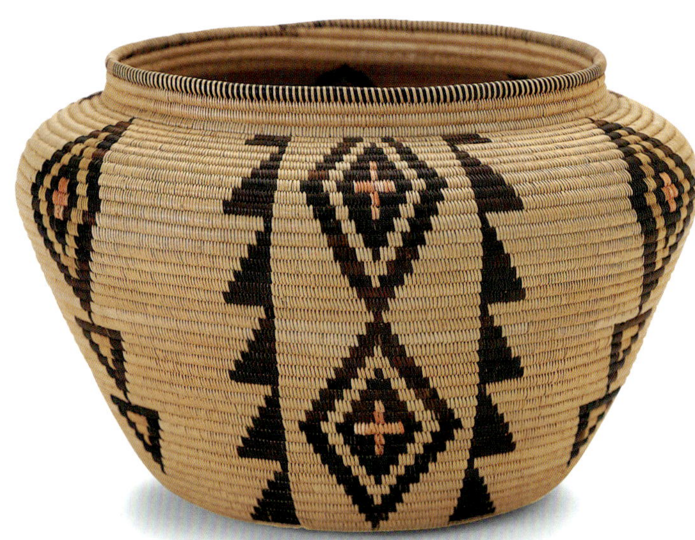

**PANAMINT BOWL BASKET, c. 1900**

5 x 7; 8 coils/inch, 31 stitches/inch. Close coiled on a grass foundation with sewing elements of willow, devil's claw and flicker feather shafts. Shown in a 1910 photo of Helen Stewart with her basket collection. Purchased by the Fred Harvey Company from the Helen Stewart estate in 1927, 289BA.

*This may be the finest stitching I have ever seen in a basket. Its perfection leaves me speechless.*

**PANAMINT BOWL BASKET, c. 1900**

4.5 x 6.5; 11 coils/inch, 45 stitches/inch. Close coiled on a grass foundation with sewing elements of willow, devil's claw and flicker feather shafts. Shown in a 1910 photo of Helen Stewart with her basket collection. Purchased by the Fred Harvey Company from the Helen Stewart estate in 1927, 291BA.

*The use of the dots on this design is unique and very effective. Museum records indicate that the woman who purchased this basket in 1920 called the dots "stars." Maybe that is what the weaver had in mind. But sometimes weavers just create designs that are striking and do not have any "meaning." What is the real story behind this striking pattern?*

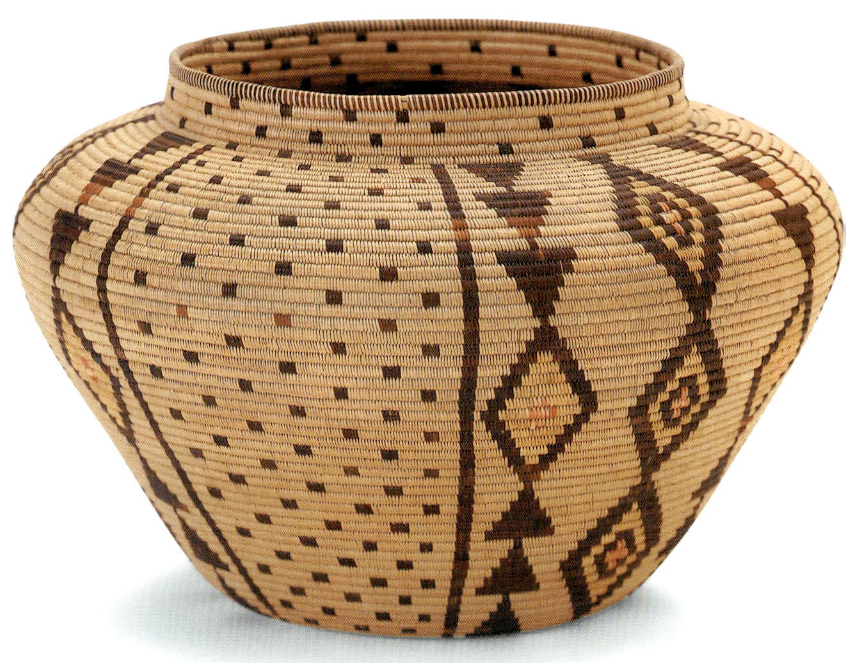

# BUILDING THE POTTERY AND BASKET COLLECTIONS

DIANA F. PARDUE

THE STRENGTH of the Heard collections is reflected in the representation of fine art from throughout North America and cultural arts from the Southwest that span the 20th century. The collection consists of items acquired by Phoenix pioneers Maie and Dwight Heard after settling in the Valley of the Sun, their subsequent acquisitions for the museum as well as generous donations by individuals and foundations from the museum's founding in March 1929 to today.

A review of the baskets and pottery in the Heard Museum collection reveals as much about the people who collected them as the people who made them. When tourists and traders invaded the West in the late 1800s, they collected Native baskets and pottery. The American Arts and Crafts Movement promoted natural products rather than industrial ones and fostered an appreciation for Native crafts, which often were used to decorate homes. All of this occurred at a time when Native peoples were increasingly being incorporated into mainstream economic systems and were searching for new sources of income.

The core collection at the Heard Museum was formed by Maie and Dwight Heard after they moved from Chicago to Phoenix in 1895, six years after the western town had become the capital of the Arizona Territory. Enamored by the arts of the Southwest, the Heards surrounded themselves with Native artwork. Baskets, textiles and pottery graced the rooms of their homes—first Buena Ranche, at McDowell Road and 51st Avenue, and then Casa Blanca, built in 1903 at Central Avenue and Monte Vista Road. Their love of Native artwork extended to Dwight Heard's office in downtown Phoenix, where Apache arts decorated the walls. By 1927, the Heards were planning to build a museum behind their Central Avenue home. It would face Monte Vista Road, then unpaved.

While public records help us construct the early years of the Heards' business and public life in Phoenix, understanding the collections they amassed often proves to be a puzzle with many pieces that, when put in place, reveal a clearer picture. Little is known about purchases prior to 1925, as the records and bills of sale at the museum date after that time. It is possible to glean some information regarding the pottery acquisitions, as well as those of the other art forms, from photographs of the interior of the Heards' home, the bills of sale, letters from Maie Heard to shop managers and, after the museum opened, to donors. Records from prior to 1940 are fragmentary since acquisition information was incomplete at the onset. The numbering system used in those records was replaced beginning in 1952, and the information contained in the original catalogues was not transferred in its entirety to the new catalogue system.

The earliest source of information for the Heard collection is a 1910 photograph album that belonged to Fred Bancroft, a cousin of Dwight Heard. The photographs reveal that the Heard home was decorated with an extensive collection of baskets and textiles as well as pottery, beadwork, jewelry, leather arts from Africa and early weapons. Although more basketry than pottery can be seen in these early black-and-white photographs of the home's interior, one dramatic image shows a Santa Clara water jar resting on the center of a table. This jar matches two ceramics in the Heard collection, one black and the other red. Each has a flared rim, and only a minuscule difference in size separates the two. The museum's early catalogue record for the red jar exclaims "very choice." Either could be the jar from the Heard home.

These catalogue records also provide a glimpse of early collecting on the part of Mr. and Mrs. Heard. They record that a canteen was collected by Dwight Heard about 1914 at the Hopi village of Walpi in Arizona. Although some information is available regarding the Heards' trips abroad, little is known about their travels within the state or the purchases made on these trips. It is thought that the Heards would at times purchase directly from Native artists, as documented in photographs of their trip to the Sudan, Africa, in 1925 and 1926. A few early photographs reveal that the Heards traveled on outings away from Phoenix, visiting prehistoric sites such as the Tonto National Historic Monument. Also, the Heards' only child, Bartlett, was an accomplished photographer who in 1914 took photographs on a family trip to the Hopi village of Walpi.

Early photographs and receipts reveal that the Heards purchased pottery and baskets from Phoenix shops such as The Curio, Vaughn's Indian Store, Graves Indian Store, and Glen Skiles Indian Craft. Baskets were also purchased from George Wharton James, a collector, author and photographer from Pasadena, California, who was a visitor to the Heard home on May 15, 1920. A small Zuni jar was presented to Mr. Heard by C. N. Cotton, Gallup, New Mexico, according to records. Cotton was a well-known promoter and salesman of Navajo textiles.

Beginning in 1925, Maie and Dwight developed an alliance with wholesale dealers Allie Walling and Herbert BraMé through their business, the Arizona Curio Company, initially based in Prescott but relocated to 39 West McDowell Road in Phoenix in 1927. The Heards paid the BraMé couple a retainer to find quality Native arts from throughout North America for the museum they were planning. The collections gathered were quite diverse and far reaching in

scope. Although receipts remain for only a few ceramics purchased from the Arizona Curio Company, a receipt dated June 12, 1928, listed separately among other purchases three large jars by the Hopi-Tewa potter Nampeyo (page 30). In the late 1800s, Nampeyo received widespread recognition for her revival of the low-shoulder jars and complex designs of the Sikyatki pottery made by ancestral Hopi from 1400 to 1625. Included in the masterworks exhibit is a large storage jar painted by Nampeyo's daughter Fannie. It was probably made with the assistance of family members in the 1930s and acquired by trader William McGee in 1948, when he purchased Tom Pavatea's store at Polacca, Arizona (page 31).

By 1940, the pottery collection begun by the Heards and now maintained by the Heard Museum was small but represented some of the outstanding work being produced at the time. It included pottery by the best-known potters of the day—Hopi-Tewa potter Nampeyo and San Ildefonso potter Maria Martinez and her painter husband, Julian. The Martinezes had developed a style of polished black pottery that was decorated with black matte paint—called black-on-black—which revolutionized pottery making in the pueblo of San Ildefonso and in the Southwest. Among the purchases acquired by the Heards were two large decorated ceramics that included a polychrome jar and a tall black-on-black vase. A third vessel is a large low-shoulder vessel that was highly polished. Although it was unsigned, the catalogue record indicated that it was the work of Maria Martinez. By 1940, the only San Ildefonso pottery that had been purchased by the Heards was made by Maria and Julian Martinez. Pottery by Maria Martinez selected for the masterworks exhibit includes a 1920s plate with a large feather design painted by Julian Martinez (page 22) and based on an early Mimbres feather design, as well as a 1970 vase with the metallic-looking "gun metal" finish and small feather pattern painted by Maria's daughter-in-law Santana (page 13).

The acquisition of pottery made by the Martinezes and Nampeyo illustrates the Heards'

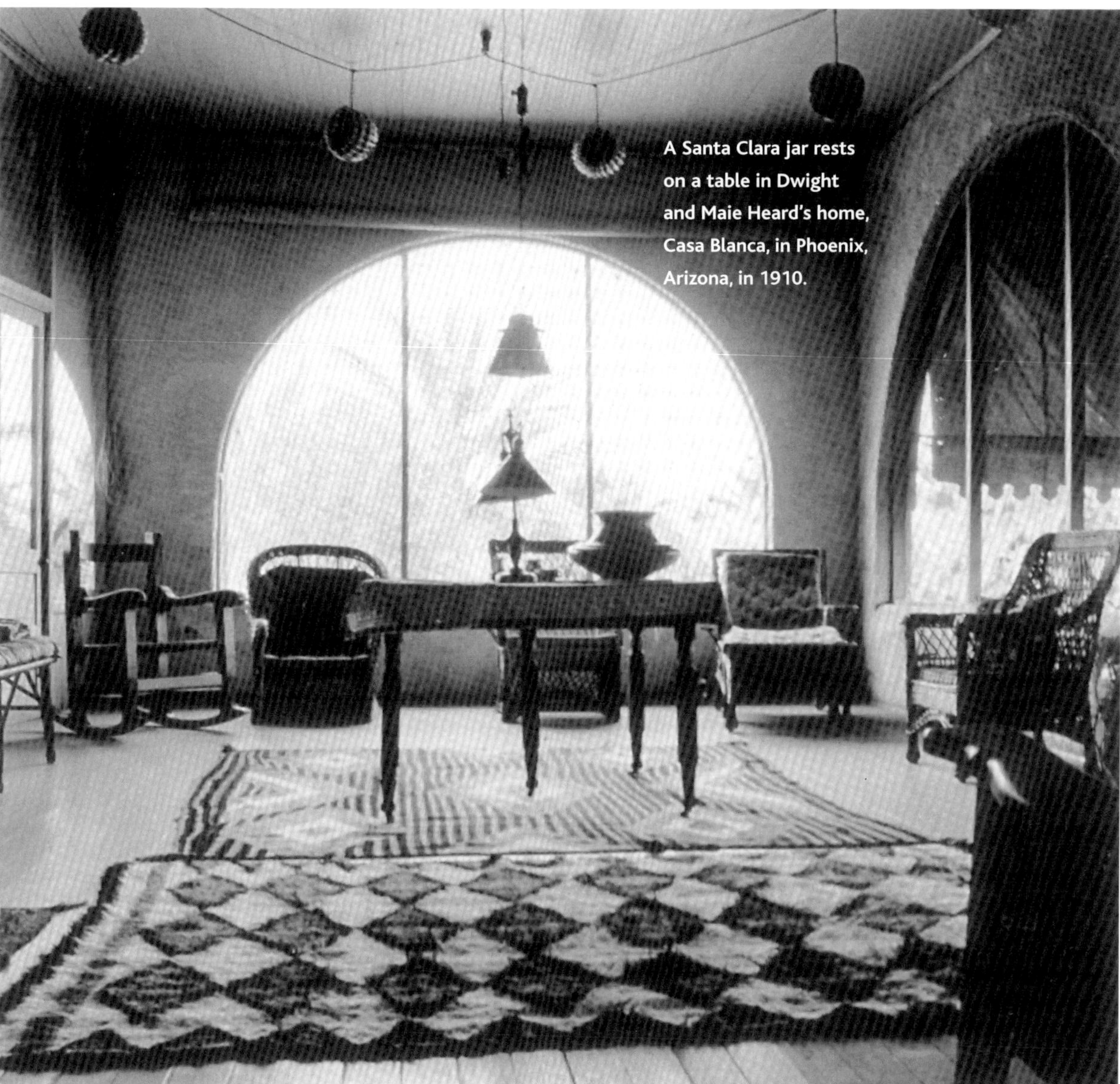



awareness of the recognition the potters had gained and also their ability to buy the best works available. They acquired additional pottery from Zuni, Acoma and Santa Clara, along with one example each from San Felipe and Santa Ana, two villages where pottery making in the early 1900s was less than prolific. With these works, the foundation of the pottery collection at the Heard Museum was established.

The Heards also sought quality baskets from throughout the West. Abe and Amy Cohn of The Emporium in Carson City, Nevada, promoted the work of Louisa Keyser, also known as Dat so la lee, creating promotional brochures and mail order catalogues that featured the artist by name. The crown jewel of any basket collection was a piece by this artist or, failing that, a superb Washoe basket by another weaver promoted to a lesser extent by the Cohns. Maie Heard purchased a collection of Washoe basketry from Herbert BraMé, that included quality works by Louisa Keyser's peers.

One prize item collected by the Heards during a 1924 trip to Hawai'i is a rare 19th-century makaloa sedge mat from the island of Ni'ihau. Collecting miniature baskets became a popular hobby for some, and Mrs. Heard acquired approximately 200 examples of these amazing baskets, the majority of which were Akimel O'odham, along with a small collection of Pomo miniatures.

At the same time Maie and Dwight Heard were developing a collection for their home, Herman Schweizer and John F. Huckle were building a collection for the Fred Harvey Company salesroom and museum at the Alvarado Hotel in Albuquerque, New Mexico. The "Indian Department," as it was called, opened in 1902 to attract tourists traveling on the Santa Fe Railway. In 1968, when the Harvey Company sold the business to Amfac Corporation, the collection of Native arts was governed by the Harvey Company Foundation until it was donated in 1978 in part to the Heard Museum and to the Museum of International Folk Art in Santa Fe, New Mexico.

Although ledger books have not been found for the Harvey Company pottery or basketry collections, it was the practice of Schweizer and Huckle to purchase from traders and dealers, to acquire large private collections and to purchase directly from artists. Records do exist at the University of Arizona Special Collections Library in Tucson for sales from John Lorenzo Hubbell of Hubbell's Trading Post in

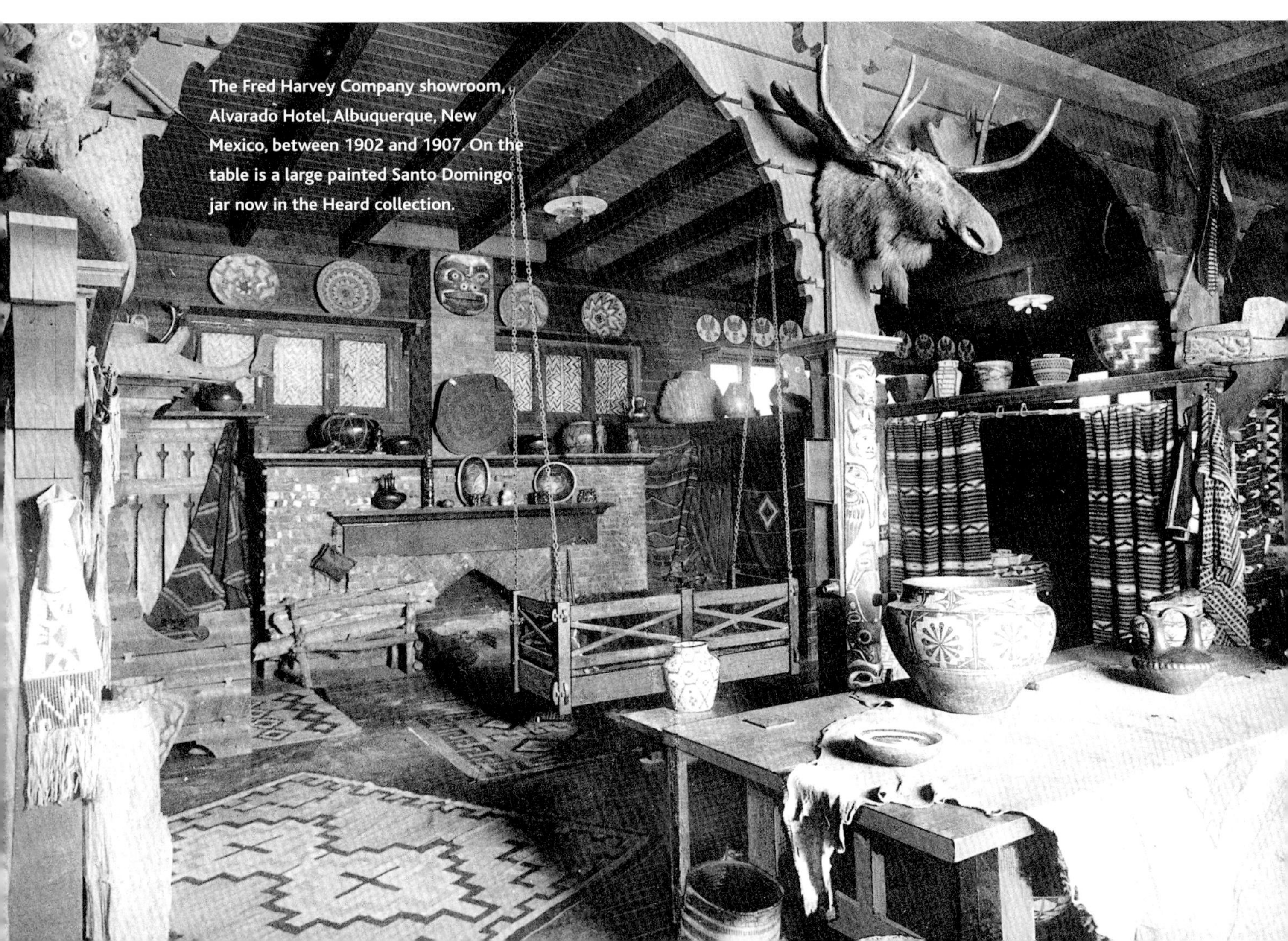

The Fred Harvey Company showroom, Alvarado Hotel, Albuquerque, New Mexico, between 1902 and 1907. On the table is a large painted Santo Domingo jar now in the Heard collection.

Ganado, Arizona, to the Harvey Company. Just as blankets were bundled, shipped courtesy of the Santa Fe Railway and sold by the pound, so were many of the Hopi ceramics. An exception to this was the sale of pottery by Nampeyo, which Schweizer and Huckle requested specifically. They also scheduled Nampeyo to demonstrate pottery making for several months at the opening of Hopi House at the Grand Canyon in 1905, again in 1907, and at the land and cattle show in Chicago in 1910. Likewise, Hubbell included a photograph of a low-shoulder jar by Nampeyo in a 1910 mail order catalogue that mentioned her name, a practice that occurred only in a few isolated instances. The Harvey Company collection retains a few examples documented as the work of Nampeyo. Among them is a series that represents the different pottery stages including a pinch pot, coiled bowl, scraped jar, polished jar and painted and fired jar. Also included in the collection are several bowls attributed by Nampeyo's great-granddaughter Dextra Quotskuyva Nampeyo as being her work. One such bowl was illustrated in several collaborative brochures produced by the Harvey Company and the Santa Fe Railway.

Records and letters prepared by collector Dr. John Hudson of Ukiah, California, shed light on many Pomo examples in the basket collections. Hudson collected baskets for both the Field Museum in Chicago and the Harvey Company, and he arranged for Pomo artists William and Mary Benson to demonstrate weaving at the Alvarado Hotel in 1904 on their way to the Louisiana Purchase Exposition in St. Louis. Several baskets that remain in the Harvey Company collection have been attributed to Mary Benson based on both technique and designs (page 54).

Maie Heard made several purchases from the Harvey Company, particularly textiles and baskets. In the 1930s, she acquired a significant Chumash lidded basket from the Harvey Company (page 56). She also purchased several Panamint baskets acquired by the Harvey Company from the collection of Helen Stewart of Nevada.

The Harvey Company collection that was donated to the museum complements the Heard collection in several important ways. The pottery and baskets are older and more extensive than those collected by the Heards, and the collection includes many Santa Ana jars from the 19th century that are diverse in shape, size and design. The collection also includes large storage jars from Santo Domingo, Santa Clara, Cochiti and Tesuque. One of the Santo Domingo jars selected for the masterworks exhibit was pictured on the table in a photograph of the Harvey Company showroom at the Alvarado Hotel taken between 1902 and 1907 (facing page; jar shown on page 30). The Harvey Company basket collection includes several Tlingit large baskets dating to 1850, a large Shasta basket, three large Pomo baskets and many fine-quality baskets of varying sizes.

When Santa Clara potter Margaret Tafoya was honored by the Heard Museum in 1994, she agreed to review the Harvey Company collection of Santa Clara pottery. She recalled having made blackware sugar bowls and creamers for the Harvey Company's La Fonda Hotel in Santa Fe, and she expected to see these small bowls and jars that were made for commercial use. Instead, large polished blackware storage jars were placed before her along with water jars and double-spouted vases. She recognized a large storage jar as one she had made and sold around 1925 (page 16), and she identified others as the work of family members including some by her mother, Sara Fina (page 16). Four of these jars, including the one Margaret Tafoya made in 1925, have been selected for the masterworks exhibit. Pottery from Zuni, Acoma and Zia pueblos are equally well represented in the Harvey Company collection.

During the Heard Museum's more than 70-year history, it has received numerous important donations. Not only are pottery and baskets from the early 1900s well represented, but also works from the 1970s onward that illustrate the shift away from artist anonymity and toward the recognition of individual artistic accomplishment. The generosity of private donors and the availability of acquisition funds have been instrumental in acquiring objects that represent the continuum of these thriving art forms.

Diana F. Pardue is Curator of Collections at the Heard Museum.

For additional reading:

*The Heard Museum History and Collections*, Ann E. Marshall and Mary E. Brennan (Heard Museum, 1989).

*Inventing the Southwest: The Fred Harvey Company and Native American Art*, Kathleen L. Howard and Diana F. Pardue (Northland Publishing, 1995).